Studying Economics

WITHDRAWN

Palgrave Study Guides

Effective Communication for Science and Technology   *Joan van Emden*
Key Concepts in Politcs   *Andrew Heywood*
Linguistic Terms and Concepts   *Geoff Finch*
Literary Terms and Criticism   *John Peck and Martin Coyle*
The Mature Student's Guide to Writing   *Jean Rose*
Practical Criticism   *John Peck and Martin Coyle*
The Student's Guide to Writing   *John Peck and Martin Coyle*
The Study Skills Handbook   *Stella Cottrell*
Studying Economics   *Brian Atkinson and Susan Johns*
Studying History   *Jeremy Black and Donald MacRaild*

How to Begin Studying English Literature (second edition)   *Nicholas Marsh*
How to Study a Jane Austen Novel (second edition)   *Vivien Jones*
How to Study Chaucer (second edition)   *Robert Pope*
How to Study a Charles Dickens Novel   *Keith Selby*
How to Study Foreign Languages   *Marilyn Lewis*
How to Study an E. M. Forster Novel   *Nigel Messenger*
How to Study a Thomas Hardy Novel   *John Peck*
How to Study James Joyce   *John Blades*
How to Study a D. H. Lawrence Novel   *Nigel Messenger*
How to Study Linguistics   *Geoff Finch*
How to Study Modern Drama   *Tony Curtis*
How to Study Modern Poetry   *Tony Curtis*
How to Study a Novel (second edition)   *John Peck*
How to Study a Poet (second edition)   *John Peck*
How to Study a Renaissance Play   *Chris Coles*
How to Study Romantic Poetry (second edition)   *Paul O'Flinn*
How to Study a Shakespeare Play (second edition)   *John Peck and Martin Coyle*
How to Study Television   *Keith Selby and Ron Cowdery*

www.palgravestudyguides.com

Studying Economics

Brian Atkinson
and
Susan Johns

palgrave

First published 2001 by
PALGRAVE
Houndmills, Basingstoke, Hampshire RG21 6XS and
175 Fifth Avenue, New York, N.Y. 10010
Companies and representatives throughout the world

PALGRAVE is the new global academic imprint of
St. Martin's Press LLC Scholarly and Reference Division and
Palgrave Publishers Ltd (formerly Macmillan Press Ltd).

ISBN 0–333–77544–9

This book is printed on paper suitable for recycling and
made from fully managed and sustained forest sources.

A catalogue record for this book is available
from the British Library.

10 9 8 7 6 5 4 3 2 1
10 09 08 07 06 05 04 03 02 01

Printed in Malaysia

Contents

List of Tables

List of Figures

Acknowledgements

The authors and publishers would like to thank the following for permission to reproduce copyright material:

David Blackaby for Table 1.1 from D. H. Blackaby, P. D. Murphy and N. C. Leary, *Graduate Earnings in Great Britain: A Matter of Degree?*, Economics Department, University of Wales.

Causeway Press Ltd for Table 2.2 from G. Rhys, 'The Motor Industry: an economic overview', *Developments in Economics*, Vol.15, ed. G. B. J. Atkinson (1999).

The Controller of her Majesty's Stationery Office for Table 2.4, data from Budget Statement 1999–2000; Table 2.2, data from 'Economic Trends' (1998); and Fig. 4.4 and Table 5.3, data from 'Family Expenditure Survey'. Crown Copyright © 2000.

Office for Official Publications of the European Communities for Table 5.2 from *Eurostatistics*, 12 (1999).

Green Books for Figs 4.1-2, adapted from *Transforming Economic Life: A Millennial Challenge*, Diagram 3, p. 20, Schumacher Briefings No.1.

Higher Education Funding Council for England for Tables 1.2–3, from C. R. Belfield *et al.*, *Mapping the Careers of Highly Qualified Workers*, HEFCE Research Series (1997).

Tim Jackson for Table 4.1, from T. Jackson, N. Marks, J. Ralls and S. Stymne. *Sustainable Economic Welfare in the UK 1950–1996*, Centre for Environmental Strategy, University of Surrey (1997).

Every effort has been made to trace all the copyright-holders, but if any have been inadvertently overlooked the publishers will be pleased to make the necessary arrangement at the first opportunity.

Introduction

We have written this book with a very clear aim: to improve your study of economics. Many students believe that the subject is hard and even dull; we believe that it is interesting, very relevant to modern life and a good basis for a career.

We have focused on students who are about to enter university to study the subject, but almost all the book will also be relevant to students embarking on courses in Further Education colleges and also Sixth-Form colleges.

The book is divided into two parts. The first part begins with a chapter on the reasons why we believe that economics is a good choice of subject. The second chapter outlines the typical content of economics courses. This is a chapter to read slowly and carefully. It will introduce you to many of the subject's fundamental concepts. Chapter 3 illustrates economics as a way of thinking and contrasts differing mainstream approaches. Chapter 4 then examines three challenges to much mainstream economics. These are Marxian, environmental and feminist. (You will notice that we have used 'she' rather than the typical 'he' in this book.) Part 1 ends with a chapter on the use of mathematics and statistics in introductory economics courses.

Part 2 of the book is concerned with learning techniques. There are chapters on topics such as study skills and how to write dissertations. Some of the ideas here will be familiar to you, but important enough to be reminded of them; other ideas will be new. Each chapter includes suggestions for further reading, and Chapter 9 includes a number of websites which you can visit to obtain information.

Several people have helped us improve this book. Bob Milward and Ian McGowan of the University of Central Lancashire, Sue Hatt of the University of the West of England, James Robertson of the New Economics Foundation and two anonymous reviewers all made very helpful comments, and we are grateful to them. In addition, Glen

Ashton gave valuable help with the manuscript. Any faults that remain are our responsibility.

Enjoy your economics!

BRIAN ATKINSON
SUSAN JOHNS

Part 1

1 Why Study Economics?

The short answer to the question 'Why study economics?' is that it is a terrific subject. Of course, we are biased; we are economists. But we think that there are three very good reasons to study economics.

- The first is that it is – or should be – interesting and that it is impossible to understand the world in which we live without some knowledge of economics.
- A second reason is that it is useful, both to the individual who studies it and also to society as a whole, since economics can lead to a better world.
- A third reason is that a qualification in economics is an excellent basis for a career.

We will examine these reasons in turn.

▶ Economics is interesting

Of course, not all economics is interesting to everyone. There are some people who are not really interested in understanding more about the world. This kind of person may well find economics boring. Similarly, not all economics is interesting, even to those who like economics. In some places, you have to *think* to get the benefit, and thinking can be hard work. If you are not in the mood to do this, then it may fail to raise your interest. Even when you are willing to work, you may find some aspects less interesting than others. For us, the most boring part of economics is that devoted to the ways in which we calculate national income and output – National Income Accounting – though others do find this interesting. Regrettably, sometimes economics fails to be interesting because its relevance is not made clear.

Economic theory is what gives the subject its strength. Subjects that lack theory are forced to become largely descriptive; this is sometimes interesting, but often shallow. The strength of economics as a subject is illustrated by the fact that it is one of the few subjects for which there is a Nobel Prize. Subjects such as law, sociology, marketing and business studies do not have this stature. Another outward sign of the strength of the subject is that economists are willing to poke fun at their subject. You can see a large selection of (very poor) 'jokes' about economics on the Internet at http://netec.mcc.ac.uk/JokEc.html. This also gives several reasons to study economics including: Mick Jagger, Arnold Schwarzenegger and Arsene Wenger all studied economics and look how they turned out

A more serious reason for studying economics is that it helps you realise when politicians are talking economic nonsense. This is not infrequent. One of the great economists of the twentieth century, John Maynard Keynes, concluded his great book *The General Theory of Employment, Interest and Money* (p. 383) by writing:

> the ideas of economists and political philosophers, both when they are right and when they are wrong, are more powerful than is commonly understood. Indeed, the world is ruled by little else. Practical men, who believe themselves to be quite exempt from any intellectual influences, are usually the slaves of some defunct economist

Understanding economics will help you recognise this.

Economic misunderstanding is widespread. Wood (1997) lists a number of fallacies. These include:

- Ticket touts are harmful
- Free trade causes unemployment
- Raising interest rates causes inflation
- Central banks can control real interest rates
- Workers should get a living wage

Though it has to be admitted that some of Wood's 'fallacies' are not accepted as fallacies by all economists, some economists would add others. For example, most economists would agree that it is a fallacy that countries should aim to be self-sufficient: that is, to produce all the goods that they consume.

A look at almost any newspaper will show you how closely economics is linked to the real world, and how we cannot really understand the context of our lives unless we have some knowledge of the subject. Some examples can illustrate this:

- How do we as a society know how many pairs of jeans to produce? How many portions of fish and chips? How much beer?
- How do firms decide the prices of their products? My little diary cost £2.50 two years ago in 1998, last year it was £3.00, this year it is £3.50 – and this at a time of very low inflation. Why?
- Why does it cost more to watch Manchester United play than it does to watch Stockport County?
- Why do (largely useless) diamonds cost more than (essential) water?

The answers to all these questions – and a million others – derive from the economists' use of demand-and-supply analysis.

Another set of questions concerns poverty and wealth. Why do (some) professional footballers earn such large sums of money, and why do people doing essential jobs such as nurses earn relatively little? Questions such as these are the domain of distribution economics, whilst questions such as 'How can we improve the environment?' and 'How can we reduce poverty?' are covered in welfare economics.

Why, and how, do firms decide to build – and close – factories? What are the best methods of deciding if an investment will be profitable? These are the domain of business and industrial economics.

Then there are questions relating to the economy as a whole. These include topics such as unemployment and inflation. And why do most economists believe in free trade, even if it means that domestic firms go out of business?

These are just a few of the questions dealt with in economics. The conclusion is clear. You cannot understand the world around you unless you have some knowledge of economics in its various aspects.

▶ Economics is useful to the individual and to society

It would be nice if we could write that studying economics will make you rich, but it simply is not true (though, as we will see, it usually does lead to good jobs). What it can do is to give you some very useful mental tools and skills that will be helpful in many other aspects of life.

Many of these skills, such as the ability to write good essays, are the subject of the second part of this book and so will not be discussed here. But there are some less obvious skills that are developed by studying economics. Some of these skills are 'overarching', such as the development of logical thought processes, whilst others are more specific to economics, such as the ability to read and interpret economic arguments.

Earlier in this chapter we mentioned that studying economics could make it possible to discover when politicians are talking nonsense. One reason why this is possible is that studying economics helps people realise the difference between statements of fact and expressions of opinion. It also helps develop a logical way of thinking about economic issues and the ability to present statements in a reasoned and relevant way. The ability to present and discuss ideas, concepts and arguments in a clear and accurate manner is an important general skill that is valuable in a wide range of careers. So is the ability to evaluate decisions, arguments and the reliability of information. This is allied to the ability to process data relating to economics, including the collection and collation of data and their use and presentation to support and illustrate arguments or points of view. Writing reports, interpreting data and analysing arguments are central to economics. If you master these skills in your study of economics you will be able to use them in a wide range of contexts, not only as a student but also in your working life.

So far we have been looking at how people who study economics can benefit. But there is a more general benefit. Whole societies can benefit from good economic policies. Low rates of unemployment, low inflation and high economic growth do not occur by chance, but because of good economic policies. These issues are discussed in detail later in the book and, as we will see, there are no easy answers. Moreover, external circumstances sometimes make it difficult to implement such policies. For example, after the break-up of the Soviet Union, political factors in Russia meant that it was not possible to implement appropriate economic policies.

The elimination – or at least reduction – of poverty can also be helped by appropriate economic policies. This is such a huge topic that we cannot possibly cover it all here. So, instead of attempting the impossible, we will illustrate the way in which economics can be useful by considering the work of one economist, Amartya Sen, who won the Nobel Prize for Economics in 1998.

Sen was born in India, and experience of the desperate poverty of the people of Bengal, particularly its women, made him keenly aware of the dehumanising effect of all who were touched by it. When he was nineteen, he came to Cambridge to study economics. Since then he has worked as an economist in several places including

Harvard University. At the time of writing he is Master of Trinity College, Cambridge.

Some of Sen's ideas are complicated and theoretical, for example, formulating ways of measuring development, but we can give an outline of some of his concerns. He argued that unregulated markets were often unsatisfactory because one person's freedom may constrain someone else. Sen argued that we need to recognise the complexity of people's choices, wants and behaviour. For example, the fact that many Bengali women collude in the subjection of their daughters does not mean that this is what they would freely choose. If we want a world where we can choose to have more or less inequality or poverty, then we need to think carefully about which inequalities we care about because dealing with one will have an impact on another.

Much of Sen's career has been about developing practical measures that boost the intellectual crusade against inequality. For Sen, it is not enough just to focus on poverty; we need to think about what poverty means for the poor. In particular, poor women are disadvantaged in that they are worse off than men in terms of diet, education and medical care. Sen has written about 100 million missing poor women, implying that politicians often behave as if these women did not exist.

Let us take a specific example: famine. The cause of famine is obvious, is it not? – there is a shortage of food.

Sen argued that this was not the fundamental cause. As he put it, 'Starvation is the characteristic of some people not *having* enough to eat. It is not the characteristic of there *being* not enough to eat' (1982, p. 1). In other words, when famine strikes, there is often enough food, but it does not reach the poor because they do not have enough money for the food that is available on the market. Thus famine can be regarded as a failure of *entitlement* – it can take place without there being a substantial decline in the availability of food, but people starve because conventional obligations and ownership rights restrict the availability of food to those in powerful positions. One solution to this is democracy, which can empower the poor and make it more difficult for the rich to corner all the food. This analysis of famine is just one aspect of the way in which Sen argues that the benefits of competitive markets are distributed unequally.

Sen is just one economist; other economists have other concerns, but his work shows how economics can be used to improve people's lives.

► Economics as a foundation for a career

For most employers, a degree is what matters; the subject is less important. Thus you will find economics graduates working in a very wide range of jobs. But economics is a subject that also leads to jobs where knowledge of the subject is very useful. Thus about one half of economics graduates go into jobs in the financial services industry. Some of these will work in the commercial banks where a degree in economics is particularly useful since it gives exemption from some bankers' examinations. This also applies to some accountancy examinations, another source of employment for many graduates in economics. Many economists also work in other sectors of the financial services industry. Insurance companies, building societies and merchant banks all employ economists. In many of these careers a knowledge of economics is combined with another area of study. In such cases, economics gives a strong theoretical underpinning to a wide range of careers.

Economists are widely employed in the public service, either as general recruits into the civil service or as specialist economists in the Government Economic Service. The senior members of this Service will advise ministers on the economic implications of alternative courses of action. The privatised utilities and the regulatory agencies such as OFWAT and OFGAS all rely on economic analysis and advice from economists and many economists also work in local government, advising on economic development. And, of course, many economists work in the education industry as teachers or lecturers (these tend to earn less than other economics graduates).

There are also jobs overseas for graduates in economics. The European Commission in Brussels and the OECD in Paris both employ a large number of economists. So do international agencies such as the World Bank and the International Monetary Fund.

Firms sometimes employ economists to make use of specialist skills such as economic forecasting, but they also employ economists because the subject gives a good grounding of skills. Since economists are literate, numerate and can analyse and evaluate, they are very useful to employers.

There is much evidence that getting a degree leads to higher salaries. For example, an economist called Psacharopoulos (1985) reviewed the research in many countries and found almost without exception that investment in higher education was a good investment, both for society as a whole and also for the individual who was educated. More recently, researchers in Britain obtained data from people aged 33. They found that the wages of both men and women with higher educational qualifications were significantly higher than those with just A-levels. Men with first degrees had hourly wages that were 21 per cent higher than those of men with just A-levels, and women with degrees had incomes 39 per cent higher than women with just A-levels, though correcting for other factors (such as ability) slightly reduced these figures (Blundell *et al.*, 1997). Similar results were obtained by Belfield *et al.* (1997). These researchers surveyed the careers of 18 000 graduates from over 40 higher education institutions. They found that by age 30–34, male graduates were earning 30 per cent more than those with A-level qualifications who did not go on to higher education. Women graduates earned even more that this compared to those women who did not go on to take a degree. So, taking a degree pays, though, of course, this does not mean that everyone who graduates will benefit. There are many exceptions, such as poorly educated individuals with high incomes and highly educated people with low incomes. The question which needs to be answered here is 'How do graduates in economics compare with graduates in other subjects?'

Four separate pieces of evidence show that on average economics graduates tend to earn considerably more than other graduates.

The first evidence is research by Dorton (1992) which examined the salaries of 1985 graduates five years after graduation. Computing graduates came top, earning 28 per cent more than the average graduate. Economists came second in his list of subjects, earning 18 per cent more than the average. Mathematics graduates earned 12 per cent more than the average whilst graduates in history earned 11 per cent less and graduates in English 12 per cent less than the average graduate.

The second piece of research is by Blackaby *et al.* (1998). This used information from a labour force survey to compare graduates in various subjects with others who had similar grades at A-level but who chose not to go to university. As suggested earlier, the results showed that it paid to take a degree. They also showed that graduates in arts subjects earned 9.4 per cent more than those who did not progress beyond A-level, whilst those taking 'economics, accountancy, law and management degrees' earned 40.8 per cent more. The researchers also compared individual degree subjects and a selection of these results are shown in Table 1.1. (It should be emphasised that this is a selection: economists earned more than average, but graduates in a few other subjects such as medicine earned more than economists.)

TABLE 1.1 GRADUATE EARNINGS IN GREAT BRITAIN BY SUBJECT (% INCREASE IN EARNINGS COMPARED WITH THOSE NOT PROGRESSING BEYOND A-LEVEL)

Economics	38%
Business and management	37%
Mathematics	32%
Mechanical engineering	27%
Biology	18%
English	15%

Source: Blackaby, D. H., Murphy, P. D., and O'Leary, N. C. (1988) 'Graduate Earnings in Great Britain: A Matter of Degree?', Economics Department, University of Wales.

Our third piece of research also comes to similar conclusions. The results are shown in Table 1.2

One reason for the differences between men and women in this particular piece of research is that the number of women sampled was relatively low and hence evidence is less strong for them. Male economics graduates were the second-highest earners, while female graduates were the fifth-highest earners. Note however, that some careers, such as law and medicine, are not included here.

Our fourth piece of evidence comes from the research mentioned earlier by Belfield and colleagues. Table 1.3 compares the earnings of 1990 economics graduates in 1996 with those who took other subjects.

TABLE 1.2 MEAN SALARIES OF 1985 GRADUATES IN 1996 BY SUBJECT (£)

Females		Males	
Electrical engineering	34686	Dentistry	41692
Mechanical engineering	33360	Economics	34971
Dentistry	33246	Management	33404
Accountancy	25225	Chemical engineering	31005
Economics	24389	Accountancy	29771
Business	22657	Physics	29552
Biology	22410	English	26842
English	21790	Geography	23345
Management	21647	Biology	22213
Politics	20946	Education	20393
Theology	16455	Theology	14243

Source: Belfield, C. R. et al. (1997) Mapping the Careers of Highly Qualified Workers, HEFCE Research Series, University of Birmingham.

TABLE 1.3   MEAN SALARIES OF 1990 GRADUATES IN 1996 BY SUBJECT (£)

Females		Males	
Dentistry	38861	Dentistry	34666
Economics	20597	Economics	22424
Accounting	22097	Accounting	22085
Geography	18739	Geography	17490
Business and Management	18103	Business and Management	21802
History	16474	History	18658
Education	17091	Education	17068

Source: Belfield, C. R. *et al.* (1997) *Mapping the Careers of Highly Qualified Workers,* HEFCE Research Series, University of Birmingham.

So, the evidence is very substantial: economists earn considerably more than those who take most other subjects. Whilst there are many exceptions, a degree in economics tends to lead to relatively higher earnings. (One reason for the different results between these investigations is that they were using different groups of graduates to obtain their figures for earnings. There were also differences in their methodology and in their sample size.)

▶ Conclusions

Economics is a good subject to study. It is interesting, and without an understanding of the subject we cannot understand the world in which we live. It develops valuable skills and so is useful for the individual, and the application of its ideas can lead to a better world. Finally, there is much evidence that it leads to good careers with relatively high earnings.

References

Belfield, C. R., Bullock, A. Chevalier, A. N., Fielding, A., Siebert, W. S., and Thomas, H. R. (1997) *Mapping the Careers of Highly Qualified Workers,* HEFCE Research Series, University of Birmingham.

Blackaby, D. H., Murphy, P. D., and O'Leary, N. C. (1988) 'Graduate Earnings in Great Britain: A Matter of Degree?', Economics Department, University of Wales.

Blundell, R., Dearden, L., Goodman, A. and Reed, H., (1997) *Higher Education, Employment and Earnings in Britain,* London, Institute for Fiscal Studies.

Dorton, P. J. (1992) 'The market for qualified manpower in the UK', *Oxford Review of Economic Policy*, vol. 8 no. 2 (Summer).

Keynes, J. M. (1936) *The General Theory of Employment, Interest and Money*, Macmillan.

Psacharopoulos, G. (1985) 'Returns to education', *Journal of Human Resources*, vol. 20 pp. 583–604.

Sen, A. (1982) *Poverty and Famines*, Oxford, Clarendon Press.

Wood, G. (1997) *Economic Fallacies Exposed*, London, Institute of Economic Affairs.

2 Typical Course Content

In this chapter we outline some of the main ideas that you will find in most economics courses. If you have not studied economics before, the ideas will be new to you and may be difficult to grasp on first reading. So, do not rush this chapter. Instead, read a section at a time and try to master the essentials.

▶ The economic problem

What is the cost to you of reading this book?

The obvious answer is the amount of money you paid for it (assuming that you bought it).

This answer might satisfy the accountant, but not an economist. For economists, the real cost of reading the book is what you could have done if you had chosen not to read the book. In other words, what could you have done with the money – and most importantly the time – if you had chosen not to read the book? There are thousands of possible alternatives, such as going to the cinema, playing sport, or going to the pub. For the economist, the real cost of reading this book is therefore the best alternative that you have given up.

This cost has a technical name in economics. It is called *opportunity cost* and can be defined as the value of the best alternative foregone when a particular action is chosen. You might not be able to measure this cost in money terms, but this approach puts a value on the resources that are needed to make possible any course of action. These resources (usually called the factors of production) include land, labour and capital. For example, if a decision is made to build a housing estate, this will require the use of land, workers and machinery. It will also require another factor of production – the efforts of an *entrepreneur*. This word was first used by a French economist called Jean Baptist Say. He defined the job of the entrepreneur as allocating resources to improve productivity; in modern economics it is usually used to describe the person who takes risks in an enterprise. Now, if these resources had not been used to build a housing estate, they could have been used for other things – perhaps to build a factory or a sports centre. The opportunity cost of the housing estate is therefore the best of these alternatives.

Let us now use this fundamental economic concept of opportunity cost to describe the fundamental economic problem. This arises because of scarcity. If we lived in a magical world, society could produce all the goods and services that people would like. But we do not live in such a world; and we can all think of things that we would like – better houses, holidays, cars, for example. But, as we have seen, if society decides to build more houses, the principle of opportunity cost means that something else has to be given up. Hence the problem of scarcity – the heart of economics -means that choices have to be made.

There are three basic questions that underlie almost the whole of economics:

1. What should we produce? Since we cannot produce everything, we have to choose: more houses or more sports centres? More cars or more public transport?
2. How should we produce these goods? For example, should we use more machinery? Should we use large-scale methods, or is small better?
3. Who should get the goods that are produced? Do we want a fairly equal society, or are there arguments for giving large rewards to those with desirable skills?

There are three possible approaches to these questions. The first is traditional: for most of human history, goods were produced and distributed using the practices that had been used for generations. Change came only slowly, so that the crops grown by one generation would be grown by its successors. This approach is not possible in a modern society that wants more goods.

A possible alternative is a planned economy. This is usually associated with the former Soviet Union and countries such as North Korea, but the UK was a planned economy during the Second World War. In a planned economy (sometimes called a command economy) the major decisions – the answers to the three questions – are made by the government; the civil service then breaks these down into orders for individual factories. Individual people also receive their orders. Whilst the UK was at war, almost all adults were told where to work or which armed service they were to join.

A planned economy has several advantages. When well-organised it means that there is little or no unemployment or inflation, and essential goods and services such as food, housing and public transport are cheap.

The system works best when the answer to 'What to produce?' is clear – in the UK it was weapons of war. But a planned economy has many disadvantages. It is bureaucratic – think of all the planners that are needed. It is also inefficient since there are few incentives to improve performance – why work harder if you are always sure of a job with similar wages? There is little freedom of choice. And planned economies cannot provide the huge range of consumer goods desired by people in a modern economy. Finally, planned economies have a poor record of innovation in production.

For these reasons, modern economies such as the UK make use of market forces – the third approach to answering our three questions.

At the heart of this approach is the consumer: the consumer is sovereign. The short answer to the question 'What to produce?' in a market economy is the goods and services that consumers are willing to buy. The second question 'How to produce?' is answered by saying that when a market works efficiently it is because producers use the most efficient system: efficient in this context means not only technical efficiency but also taking into account the costs of various methods of production. The answer to 'Who gets the goods?' is that they go to those willing to pay, and economic rewards in a market go to those with skills, goods or services that people are willing and able to buy. The whole system works without any great bureaucracy and leads to high living standards and a wide choice of goods for the consumer. In other words, markets are an efficient way to produce the goods and services that people really want.

However, pure market systems do have faults: for example, there are often periods of high unemployment and those without saleable skills can lead lives of poverty. Hence in many countries there is a mixture: extensive use of markets is combined with government intervention in the economy. This approach is the focus of almost all introductory courses in economics and many of the issues we have briefly mentioned here are explored in detail in the rest of this book.

▶ Typical content for the early part of the course

There are hundreds of courses in economics, so obviously there are differences between them. Despite this, there is a central core that will be found in almost all introductory economics courses.

Most will begin with a discussion along the lines described above before introducing two central concepts that are as essential to economics as addition and subtraction are to arithmetic. These concepts are *demand* and *supply*, and it is important that you master them because they can be used in a huge range of situations, from analysing the price and quantities of goods produced and the causes of unemployment, to the value of a currency.

Let us begin with demand. Like many words in economics, it has a precise meaning that differs from that in everyday life where it can mean 'want'. For economists, however, 'demand' only exists when people are willing to pay for a good. To take an extreme example, you could be dying of thirst in the desert, but if you do not have enough money to pay for a drink, then, economically, you have no demand for water. Hence, demand is desire for a good, backed up by willingness to pay, so that it can usually be measured by how much consumers actually pay. If consumers spend £x million on a good each week, then we can say that weekly demand for that good is £x million. The only exception to this rule occurs when consumers are willing to buy but the good is not available, for example because of a strike.

Now what determines the quantity of a particular good that you are willing to buy? One obvious factor is the price. If beer cost £1000 a pint, we would drink something else. Hence we might expect that demand will fall as price rises, whilst price cuts will entice consumers to buy more. Other factors that might affect the demand for a particular good include the level of consumers' incomes – rich people will buy more goods irrespective of the price. Other factors that affect demand include advertising and the price and quality of other goods.

The other crucial concept is supply. This is a bit more difficult because we are all familiar with buying, but relatively few of us are producers. By 'supply' economists mean the quantity of a good or service that firms are willing to make available at various prices in a given time period. Again, the most important determinant of supply is price. At higher prices we might expect firms to be willing to make more goods available since higher prices are likely to mean higher profits and higher prices mean that firms will be able to increase output, for example by putting workers on overtime. Conversely, at very low prices, firms may not be willing to supply any goods at all. In addition to price, other factors that affect supply are firms' costs, such as the level of wages and the price of raw materials. Changes in technology will also affect firms' willingness to supply goods at a particular price.

Equilibrium

It is now time to bring together demand and supply. This interaction is the basis of a huge amount of economic analysis, so it is important that you master it.

In order to do this we will examine the relationship between demand and price and supply and price, and for the moment assume that other factors are unchanged. This assumption is called *ceteris paribus* – literally, 'other thing being equal'.

We have seen that a low price means higher demand and lower supply whilst high prices are associated with a fall in demand and greater supply. We can show these relationships in a table, and this is done hypothetically for T-shirts in Table 2.1.

Let us examine this table. It shows that as price rises fewer T-shirts will be demanded and more will be supplied. At a price of £7 demand will equal supply. This is called the equilibrium price. Every consumer willing to pay this price will be able to purchase a T-shirt. Also at this price, firms will be able to sell all that they produce. The market will clear; there will be no surpluses and no shortages.

At any other price there will be either shortages or surpluses, but the price system will work to clear these. For example, if the price were £3, demand would be much greater than supply and shortages would occur. Since many consumers would be willing to pay more than this price, firms would have an incentive to put up their prices. As you can see from the table, this would choke off some demand from those not

TABLE 2.1 DEMAND AND SUPPLY OF T-SHIRTS

Price (£)	Demand (thousands per month)	Supply (thousands per month)
3	10	2
5	8	4
7	6	6
9	4	8

willing to pay the higher price; it would also be an incentive for firms to increase supply. Eventually, the price would rise until demand equalled supply.

Similarly, if the original price were very high, firms would not be able to sell all that they produced; they would have to cut the price to entice consumers to buy. The price would continue to fall until equilibrium was reached at a price of £7, when 6000 T shirts would be produced and sold.

This relationship between demand (D) and supply (S) can be shown in a diagram, and this is done in Figure 2.1. This is probably the most famous diagram in the whole of economics, and is worth studying carefully because this basic diagram is adaptable to many other economic situations.

The diagram shows two curves. The demand curve tells us how much will be demanded at a range of prices. It slopes down from left to right showing that more will be bought at lower prices. The supply curve shows how many T-shirts' firms will be willing to supply at a range of prices. It slopes upwards from left to right. The two curves meet at a price of £7 – the equilibrium price. Above this price, supply is greater

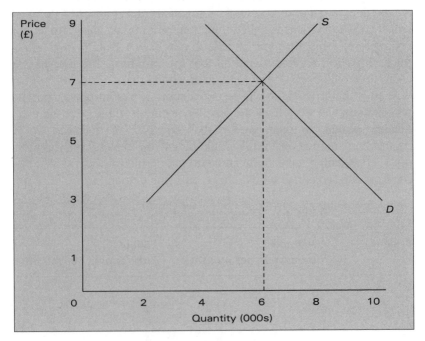

FIGURE 2.1 DEMAND, SUPPLY AND EQUILIBRIUM

than demand and surpluses occur. Below the equilibrium price, demand is greater than supply and if they want to increase their profits, firms will put up the price until it reaches equilibrium. In this way, market forces answer our basic question – what (and how much) to produce. The interaction of demand and supply has worked to clear the market.

Shifts in curves

So far we have assumed *ceteris paribus* – that other factors are unchanged. But what if other factors do change?

Let us look in a bit more detail at the factors that determine demand. We can put these into the form of an equation:

Demand = f (price, income, advertising, price and quality of other goods . . .)

This equation shows these other factors. The 'f' means that demand is a function of (is determined by) the things that follow in the equation (the dots show that there might be factors other than those listed). Let us examine just one of these factors. For example, we might expect that a rise in consumers' incomes would mean that consumers would be willing to buy more T-shirts at all prices. We show this on our basic diagram by adding a new demand curve. Put another way, there has been a shift in the demand curve. This is shown in Figure 2.2. In this diagram we have not used numbers as in Figure 2.12, but instead used letters such as p^1 to represent the original price, p_2 to show the second price level and similarly q_1 and q_2 to show original and subsequent levels of the quantity. This is a common technique used in economics texts.

The result of this shift in the demand curve is that there is a new equilibrium. This is at a higher price – a movement from the original price p_1 to p_2. The diagram also shows that more goods will be sold, in this case from the original q_1 to q_2. Figure 2.2 shows the effect of a rise in consumer incomes. A similar result would occur as a result of a successful advertising campaign. More would be demanded at each price. On the other hand, some changes such as a fall in incomes, perhaps because of a recession or a rise in income tax, would have the opposite effect. The demand curve would shift to the left as shown in Figure 2.3. The result: prices would fall from p_1 to p_2 and the quantity manufacturers sell would also fall, from q_1 to q_2.

Changes in the other components in our equation would also shift the demand curve. For example, a new competing product would shift

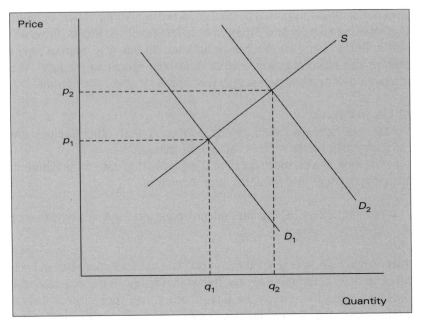

FIGURE 2.2   A SHIFT IN THE DEMAND CURVE – THE EFFECT OF A RISE IN CONSUMERS' INCOME

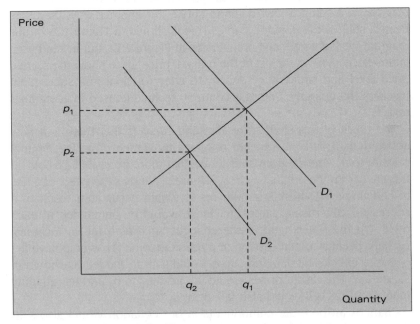

FIGURE 2.3   THE EFFECT OF A FALL IN INCOMES

the demand curve of our original T-shirt manufacturer to the left, and the result would be similar to that shown in Figure 2.3.

Shifts in curves and movements along curves

One of the most common errors made by students is that they fail to distinguish between a movement *along* a curve and a movement *of* the entire curve. Let us examine the difference. A good starting point is our demand equation:

Demand = f (*price*, income, advertising, price and quality of other goods . . .)

A change in price causes a movement along the curve. In our original example (Figure 2.1) a change in the price of T-shirts caused such a movement. When the price of a good falls, the movement is down the curve. When price rises, the movement is up the curve.

However, changes in all the other factors apart from price cause the whole curve to shift – the reason why we differentiated price from the other factors by putting it in italics. For example, if the good in question is a particular model of Ford cars, then the arrival of a competing new model from a rival manufacturer will cause the entire curve to shift to the left as shown in Figure 2.4. This means that fewer cars will be demanded at every price. The result is that Ford can expect to sell fewer cars at a lower price. This is an example of a competitive or substitute good affecting another product.

[Note that in all these examples I have drawn a rough diagram. This is a very good practice to adopt. Whenever you are thinking about demand and supply, rough out a simple diagram.]

Just as the demand curve can shift, so can the supply curve. Just as we wrote a demand equation, so we can write an equation which lists some of the factors affecting supply:

Supply = f (*price*, technology, wages, raw materials, weather . . .)

Again, price is in italics because it is different from all the other factors. A change in price means a movement along the curve. On the other hand, all the other factors mean that the whole curve shifts. For example, the introduction of a new machine will cut costs and mean that firms are willing and able to supply more at the same price – this is shown by a shift of the entire supply curve as shown in Figure 2.5. The result is that there is a fall in price from p_1 to p_2 whilst the quan-

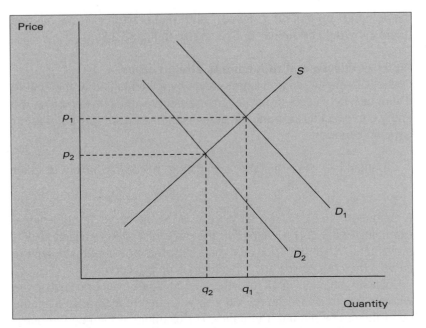

FIGURE 2.4   THE EFFECT OF A NEW SUBSTITUTE GOOD

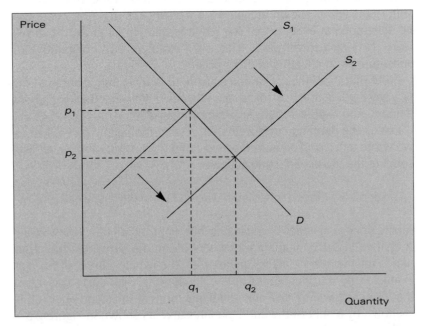

FIGURE 2.5   A SHIFT IN THE SUPPLY CURVE – THE EFFECT OF BETTER MACHINES

tity rises from q_1 to q_2. A fall in raw material prices will also cut costs and have the same effect. On the other hand, an increase in wages will mean that firms are unable to supply the same quantity of goods at the original prices – the supply curve in this example will shift to the left.

Since it is so fundamental, let us summarise this section. In a market economy, the quantity of a good that is produced and consumed will be determined by price; in turn, that is determined by the forces of demand and supply. For example, a higher price will stimulate output but deter consumers. A lower price will cause people to want to buy more of the good, but suppliers will produce smaller amounts. At some point, these forces will converge towards equilibrium. At this price, the market will clear; every consumer willing to pay the price will be able to buy the good, and firms will be able to sell all they produce.

Elasticity
Think back to our original three questions. So far we have been concentrating on the first question – what goods and services to produce. Our answer has been that in a market economy this is deter-mined by the interaction of demand and supply. But we need to intro-duce another concept before we leave this subject. This is *elasticity*.

In our diagrams so far we have drawn our demand and supply curves at roughly 45 degrees. This is a simplification. In real life a change in price will sometimes have a big effect on the quantity of goods a consumer is willing to buy; at other times it will have only a tiny effect.

Some examples will clarify this. Imagine that there is a rise in the price of toilet rolls. Do you refuse to buy so many? The answer is surely no; the same is true for changes in the price of goods such as light bulbs, salt, paper clips and envelopes. These are all goods where there are no close substitutes and where they make up only a small part of our total spending. In cases such as these we say that demand is inelastic as shown in Figure 2.6. In other words, when demand is inelastic, a large change in price will have only a proportionally small effect on the quantity demanded.

The result will be quite different for goods where there are close substitutes or where a large part of total spending is required to buy the good. A particular brand of jeans is a good example; if consumers believe that most brands are similar, then a rise in the price of one brand will lead to a relatively large fall in sales. The same is true for compet-ing brands of washing machines, cars and CD players. In all these cases, we can say that demand is elastic as shown in Figure 2.7. (Note that these figures have different scales. This is to emphasise the effect.)

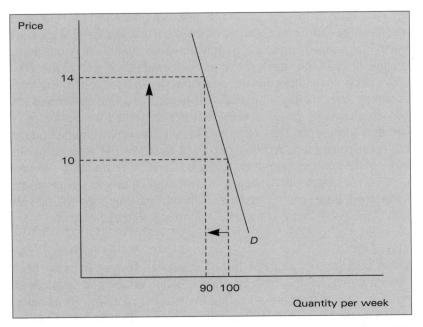

FIGURE 2.6   INELASTIC DEMAND – A LARGE CHANGE IN PRICE HAS ONLY A SMALL EFFECT ON QUANTITY DEMANDED

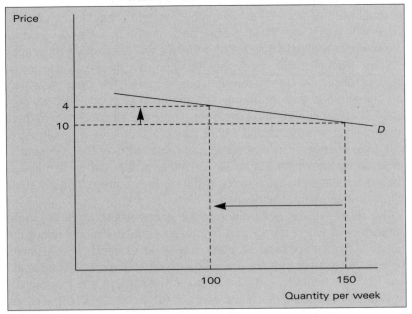

FIGURE 2.7   ELASTIC DEMAND – A SMALL CHANGE IN PRICE HAS A LARGE EFFECT ON QUANTITY DEMANDED

The importance of elasticity is that a price change will have very different effects for the firms depending on whether demand is elastic or inelastic. An example will show this.

Consumers tend to think that all petrol brands are very similar, so demand for a particular brand, such as Shell or Esso, is very elastic. In situations like this, firms will constantly try to cut their prices since the result of a small fall in price will be many more sales. That is why petrol stations advertise their petrol prices in fractions of a penny.

Diagrams are a convenient way of illustrating elasticity; for more precision, however, we need a mathematical formula which measures the relationship between changes in price and the corresponding changes in output.

So far we have been discussing elasticity of demand; the identical concept for supply is called elasticity of supply. Sometimes this is inelastic. For example, for many agricultural products it is difficult or impossible to increase supply until the next season, even if there is a huge rise in price. If someone invented a coconut slimming diet, there might be a huge rise in demand for coconuts, but since supply is inelastic, the result would be a rise in price from p_1 to p_2 whilst quantity would hardly change, rising only from q_1 to q_2 as illustrated in Figure 2.8.

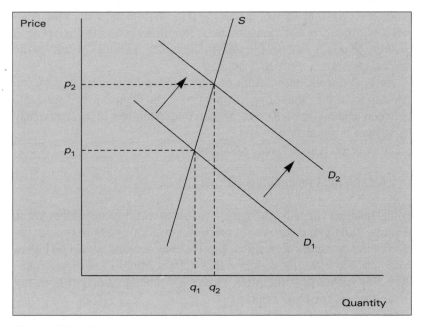

FIGURE 2.8   THE EFFECT OF AN INCREASE IN DEMAND WHEN SUPPLY IS INELASTIC

manufactured products, however, supply is elastic. A rise in make it possible for manufacturers to increase output, for by putting workers on overtime or by recruiting more workers. In this case, elastic supply means that a rise in demand will have a relatively large effect on quantity, but the change in price will be relatively small.

We have spent quite a lot of time discussing demand, supply and elasticity. That is because these are fundamental concepts which permeate almost the whole of economics and which are immensely valuable if you want to understand the world in which we live. For example, why are taxes high on alcohol and tobacco? The answer is that demand is inelastic, so that the price rise caused by the tax has relatively little effect on sales. Hence the tax does not unduly harm the firm, and the government gets a large amount of tax revenue.

Another example: why can Coca-Cola charge a higher price for its product than other cola manufacturers? Answer: consumers believe that it is different from other colas, so demand for Coca-Cola is inelastic, meaning that a high price has only a small detrimental effect on sales.

Costs and revenue

So far we have been concentrating on our first big question – 'What to produce?' Our brief answer is that the price system influences the decisions of producers and consumers so that firms produce the type and quantity of goods that people are willing to buy. Let us now turn to the second question – 'How to produce?'

Our big concept here is that of cost and we have already explored one aspect of this, that of opportunity cost. But economists distinguish between several types of costs, and an understanding of these can help us answer our question.

Let us begin with a simple equation:

Profit = total revenue – total cost

Total revenue usually increases as sales rise: more sales, more revenue. But the increase is not proportional. Think back to our discussion of the demand curve which showed that demand would be higher when price is low. This suggests that if firms want to sell more goods, they may have to cut the price. Hence a doubling of output does not mean that revenue will double.

Total cost will also be related to the quantity of goods sold; it obviously costs more to produce many goods than a few. However, some-

TABLE 2.2   OPTIMUM SCALE IN VARIOUS CAR-MAKING ACTIVITIES

	Output per year
Casting of engine block	1 000 000
Power train (engine, transmission etc.)	600 000
Pressing of various panels	1–2 000 000

Source: Rhys, G. (1999) 'The Motor Industry: An Economic Overview', in Atkinson, G. B. J. (ed.), *Developments in Economics*, Vol. 15, Causeway Press.

times doubling output means that costs rise by less than double. In this case we say that there are economies of scale. In other words, there are advantages in producing on a large scale. The car industry is a good example. Table 2.2 shows the optimum scale of production for making cars. Below these levels of output, costs will be relatively high.

This suggests that for car makers, costs will be relatively high until they produce at least 600 000 of each model of car. Up till this point there will be considerable economies of scale suggesting that, in this case, the answer to the question 'How to produce?' is 'On a large scale'.

Underlying this analysis are two other concepts of cost, those of average cost and marginal cost. In this context, we can define average cost as total cost divided by the quantity. Hence if the total cost of producing 100 items is £1000, the average cost is £10.

Marginal cost is a little more complicated. The idea of 'marginal' is crucial in economics and it is used in a wide range of contexts. Essentially, when we use this term we are saying, 'What will be the result if we make a small change?' In the case of costs, if the total cost of producing 100 items was £1000 and the total cost of producing 101 items was £1005, then the marginal cost of the 101st item was five pounds. So we can define marginal cost as the cost of producing one additional item.

The notion of marginal revenue is very similar. If a firm's total revenue from selling 100 items is £1000 and its total revenue from selling an additional item is £1005, then the marginal revenue from selling this additional item is £5. Hence we can define marginal revenue as the additional income received by a firm from selling an additional item.

Let us put together these two concepts, marginal cost and marginal revenue. I want to do this because this leads to a very important result: *a firm will maximise its profits if it increases output up to the point at*

TABLE 2.3 MARGINAL COST AND MARGINAL REVENUE

Quantity	Marginal cost (£)	Marginal revenue (£)
10	–	–
11	35	38
12	30	32
13	25	26
14	20	20
15	25	14
16	30	6

which marginal cost equals marginal revenue. Table 2.3 explains this conclusion.

Let us look at this table. It shows what happens to a hypothetical firm's marginal cost and revenue as it expands output. Its marginal cost falls at first because it is benefiting from economies of scale. However, there comes a point, in this case at an output of 14 items, when diseconomies set in and marginal cost starts to rise.

Marginal revenue is different. This firm has to keep cutting its prices if it wants to sell more – that is, it is faced with a demand curve that slopes down in the usual way.

Now put the two together. When the firm expands its output from 10 to 11 items, the cost of this eleventh item will be £35; selling this item will bring in £38. Consequently, it will pay the firm to expand output. Similarly, increasing output from 11 to 12 items will cost an extra £30 and bring in £32 more revenue. Again, this expansion will be profitable. When we expand output to 14 items the revenue brought in and the extra cost will be the same – £20. This is the most profitable level of output, because if the firm continues to increase production, to 15 items, its costs will rise by £15 whilst selling this item will only bring in £14. Expanding output to this level is therefore not profitable. Hence we can conclude that it will pay a firm to expand output until the point is reached when marginal revenue equals marginal cost. This is an important conclusion that can also be shown in a diagram. This is done in Figure 2.9.

As you can see, the marginal cost curve is 'U'-shaped. Economics textbooks often use this shape to illustrate marginal cost, but in real life, of course, it is never as regular as this.

The firm's marginal revenue curve slopes down, showing that it has

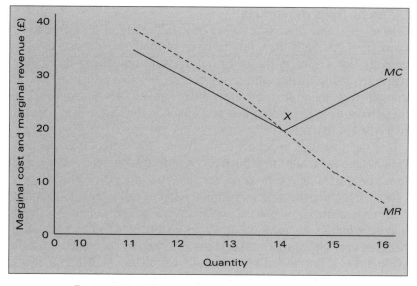

FIGURE 2.9   MARGINAL COST AND MARGINAL REVENUE

to cut its prices if it wishes to sell more goods. The firm will maximise its profit if it expands output until marginal revenue equals marginal cost, at point X. Until this point is reached the revenue brought in by expanding output will exceed the cost. After this point, the costs will exceed the revenue.

[A note for the very critical. You may ask why the firm should expand output to the point where marginal cost *equals* marginal revenue – in this example 14 items – since this item does not bring in any additional profit. The answer is that economists' definition of cost differs from the one we use in everyday life. Economists include in their definition of costs a notional element of profit needed to keep the firm in business. If the firm were not making some profit, it would be rational to close down the firm and invest money somewhere else. Hence, in our example, we have included this notional element of profit in cost, so at item 14, the firm is actually making a little profit. Do not worry if you think this is esoteric and complicated – it is!]

Now all this discussion of marginal cost and marginal revenue may seem a bit removed from real life. Whilst it is true that firms' executives may not use these terms, rational decision-making will mean that they do ask, 'Will it be profitable for us to expand output?' This is really the question we have been analysing.

Different types of markets

One of the most important topics you will study in an introductory economics course is the different types of market that exist. In some markets, for example, those for hairdressing and home decorating, there are many buyers and many sellers. In others such as aircraft manufacture, there are only a few buyers and sellers. Factors such as these have a big effect on prices and quantity. Here we will just look at two types of market.

One type is called imperfect competition. This market is competitive in that there are many firms, but it is not perfectly competitive since each firm's product is different; economists call this product differentiation.

Imperfect competition is very common in the real world; for example, it is characteristic of pubs, plumbers, and painters. Hairdressing is another example. My local Yellow Pages has about 400 entries for ladies' hairdressers – clearly this market is characterised by competition. But the competition is not perfect because each hairdresser is different. This is shown by their names, such as Bangs, Head First, Head to Head, and Blondes on Top. These names suggest that their products are different. These characteristics of imperfect competition mean that prices and profits tend to be low – unless the firm can convince customers that their product is different in which case they can charge higher prices. However, this may not be for long since other firms will follow any innovation.

Oligopoly is probably the most important kind of market. The word comes from the Greek word meaning few, and oligopolistic industries are characterised by having only a few firms. There are many examples. The oil business is dominated by a few very large firms such as Esso, Shell and BP. A walk down any High Street will show that a few firms dominate the banking industry. So do a few firms in car manufacturing and supermarkets.

The essential feature of an oligopolistic industry is that the actions of one firm will affect the others in the industry. For example, before Esso decides to cut its prices, it has to consider what its rivals will do. If they did nothing, then Esso may gain a bigger market share. However, if its competitors follow suit, then consumers will benefit from lower prices all round, but Esso will not benefit at all since it will not have managed to increase its market share. There is therefore pressure to collude in oligopolistic markets. If all oil companies got together, they could push up the price and still sell nearly as much oil. That is why this type of collusion is illegal. Despite this, various kinds of collusion do take place; for example, firms may divide up the market by agreeing not to sell their product in certain areas.

Oligopoly is characterised by a great deal of product differentiation; particularly in the form of advertising. If it is successful, advertising has two benefits for the firm. It will shift the demand curve to the right and it makes it more inelastic if it persuades customers that the product is better than its competitors'. Coca-Cola is an example that we have already mentioned, and a survey of television adverts will show that most are placed by firms in oligopolistic industries.

Distribution – the 'who' question

So far we have looked at our first two questions – what and how to produce. It is now time to look at the third question: 'Who should get the goods and services that are produced?'

In a market economy, the owners of a firm receive their rewards as profits. These will depend on several factors. For example, is the industry competitive? In a competitive industry we should expect firms to make only normal profits. If excessively large profits are being made, then new firms will enter the market, and this increase in supply will force down the price. Of course, this may take a very long time since it is difficult for new firms to enter into some industries. For example, Microsoft makes the operating systems of most computers. Challengers to this domination find it very difficult to compete, so Microsoft's profits continue to grow.

Another factor which will affect profits will be the efficiency of the firm. We can distinguish between two types of efficiency. 'X-efficiency' is a rather posh term for the way we think of efficiency in everyday life. A firm is X-efficient if it keeps down its costs of production whilst maintaining quality and quantity. If it can do this, its profits will be higher than those of competitors with higher costs. The other aspect of efficiency, which is often applied to economic systems as a whole as well as to individual firms, is called distributional efficiency: does the firm produce the goods that consumers actually want? Again, if its products are valued, then profits will be relatively high. In all these aspects the quality of the entrepreneur is vital; good managers/innovators will cause firms to have higher profits than firms with poor ones.

But what about the workers?

Here there is some disagreement among economists. The traditional view is that workers will earn what they are worth to the firm. If an additional, that is, marginal worker is employed, and each week this worker produces output that sells for £200, then it will be worth employing this additional worker so long as the wage (and other costs) do not exceed £200. The notion is the same as we saw earlier which said that a firm would maximise profit if it expanded output till marginal revenue equals marginal cost. In the case of employment, this line of thought is adapted to say that a firm will employ more and more workers until the revenue that they produce equals their marginal cost (that is, their wages plus other employment costs such as employers' National Insurance contributions).

So, in this approach, workers' earnings will depend on the quantity and value of the output that they produce. People with an output that is highly valued in the market will receive high wages; those whose output is not worth much in the marketplace will receive only low wages.

This approach is criticised by some economists. They argue that it is impossible for employers to calculate the value of workers' output and that, in any case, firms in markets where competition is limited can exploit their workers by charging high prices for their products and keeping some of this money as excess profits rather than passing it on as wages. Moreover, many workers do not have an output that is sold. How can we even attempt to measure the output of police officers, nurses or teachers?

Whatever the truth of these criticisms, there is no doubt that in many cases there is a close link between workers' productivity and their earnings. So, a summary answer to our question 'Who gets what is produced?' would be workers whose output is highly valued by the market.

Market failure
Probably the 'big' question in economics is deciding what should be left to the working of the market and when the government should intervene to correct market failure. In some cases, there is considerable agreement, for example, when an industry is characterised by monopoly. Then the government should intervene to protect consumers. Similarly, there are some goods such as defence, law and order and the provision of streets and street lighting that cannot be provided efficiently by markets. One reason for this is that it is not possible to prevent people from benefiting even if they have not paid for the good or service. You cannot have barriers at every street junction to charge people on entry. Hence providing streets cannot be profitable and private firms will not provide such services (though there are some privately owned roads and bridges that charge consumers). That is why in every country services such as defence are provided by the

government, though of course particular aspects of defence can be contracted out to private firms by the government. There is less agreement about other aspects of market failure. For example, many economists believe that if we left education, health and the provision of parks and libraries to the market, consumers would not buy enough of these goods. Consequently, the state intervenes in these markets to provide these 'merit' goods. Conversely, they also intervene to reduce consumption of goods that are considered undesirable such as alcohol, tobacco and other drugs. In other words, governments take the view that consumer sovereignty leads to results that are undesirable in some way.

Another area where markets fail concerns 'externalities'; these occur when the activities of a person or firm spill over and affect others not involved in the decision. For example, someone with an infectious disease might not get it treated; this would then be passed on to others. Consequently, the state intervenes to provide both treatment and prevention, say by inoculation. Pollution is another area where externalities exist. When people drive cars they cause pollution and congestion and increase the likelihood of accidents. Hence, the state intervenes to discourage this by taxing cars and by subsidising public transport. Externalities are also the reason why we need to get planning permission before we can build new houses or factories.

Information failures can also cause markets to fail. In the modern world, many products are so complicated that we cannot judge their true value. Second-hand cars are a good example; few people can judge if they are safe. Hence garages selling such cars have to comply with many regulations, as do builders. For the same reason, there are many regulations concerning food safety.

So, despite the huge benefits which markets bring, they do not solve all economic problems; we need governments and government action.

▶ The second part of the course – macroeconomics

So far we have been talking about *micro*economics – the economics of (relatively) small-scale economic activity. Now we need to move on to the *macro*, that is, the study of the economy as a whole. This deals with very important questions such as the causes and cures of unemployment and inflation, how countries can achieve economic growth and the advantages and possible disadvantages of international trade.

In order to examine these kinds of questions, we need a bit of background. Just as accountants examine firms' accounts, so economists look at the accounts of the country as a whole. Not surprisingly, these are called national income accounts. There are three ways to do this, and in principle they should all give the same result. The first way is to add together the total output of the economy, that is, the output of all the firms in the country plus the notional output of industries such as education, health and defence. This gives us a figure for gross national product, usually shortened to GNP. Output gives rise to incomes. If someone buys furniture for £100, this is the value of the output and the money goes to someone, for example, as wages, rent or profit. Hence national output must equal national income. Similarly, when the furniture is sold we can look at who buys it – for example, consumers, or the government. These three ways of examining the national accounts form the background to macroeconomics. The details of how they are constructed can be rather complex so I am not going to elaborate here except to say that such complex calculations can never be entirely accurate.

Macroeconomic concerns also affect our three original questions. For example, one answer to the question 'What to produce?' would be 'relatively little when there is a recession'. On the other hand, when incomes are rising because the economy is booming, people will choose more luxury goods. Similarly, when unemployment is high, part of the answer to the question 'Who gets the goods that are produced?' would be that many people will be able to afford only a few goods.

Aggregate demand (AD) and aggregate supply (AS)
There are a number of different approaches to learning macroeconomics, but perhaps the most useful is to develop the microeconomic concepts of demand and supply. In the macro context these change and become aggregate demand and aggregate supply.

Aggregate demand is the amount of money which people wish to spend in the domestic economy. Because it is concerned with domestic spending, it includes exports (since the money from these benefits the domestic economy) but excludes imports (since the money goes abroad). Its components can most conveniently be shown as an equation:

$$AD = C + I + G + X - M$$

where AD is aggregate demand, C consumption, I investment, G government spending, X exports and M imports.

As we will see in the next chapter, economics is really a way of thinking rather than a list of things to be learnt, but this equation is perhaps an exception and is worth remembering.

Let us explore each component in a bit of detail.

As its name implies, consumption is spending by consumers. It includes not only goods such as food and clothing, but also services such as holidays, insurance and banking. It is easily the largest component of aggregate demand. In an ideal world we would be able to predict consumers' spending because this would allow firms to plan how much to produce; moreover, governments could take action if spending was going to fall, perhaps causing a recession, or if spending was expected to rise substantially, perhaps causing inflation. Unfortunately, consumer spending is difficult to predict. Its main determinant is probably income after tax (which economists call 'disposable income'), because when incomes rise we tend to spend more. But there are other factors affecting consumer spending. Age is a factor; for example, students usually tend to spend all their income and then whatever they can borrow.

Investment is also difficult to predict, and spending on this component of aggregate demand fluctuates considerably from year to year. By 'investment' we mean spending by firms on such items as factories, offices, vehicles, machinery and raw materials. (Investing in a building society or bank is not investment in this context; instead economists classify this as saving.) Expectations play a part in determining investment. If firms think that the future is rosy, they will be willing to spend money on expansion. Another factor affecting the level of investment is the rate of interest. Firms often borrow to finance their investment. Hence high interest rates will increase the cost, so investment will fall. On the other hand, low interest rates will tend to encourage investment

Table 2.4 shows the main items of public spending. Not all these contribute to aggregate demand since some items such as most spending on social security are 'transfer payments'. In other words, money is taken from some people as tax and given to others. Money spent on such things as books or roads is counted as part of aggregate demand.

The other two items of aggregate demand – exports and imports – are also affected by the level of national income. When incomes rise, we spend more on imports, for example, by buying more electronic goods made abroad and by going on foreign holidays. Similarly, exports will rise when foreign incomes are growing. It is therefore beneficial to the UK when other countries' living standards are rising since they will buy more of our goods, so raising income and employment in the UK.

TABLE 2.4 PUBLIC EXPENDITURE 1999–2000

	£ billion
Social security	102
Health	61
Education	41
Defence	22
Law and order	19
Industry, agriculture and employment	15
Housing & environment	13
Transport	9
Debt interest	26
Other spending	41
Total	349

Source: HM Government Budget Statement.

Table 2.5 shows the relative contributions of the different parts of aggregate demand.

A word about tables such as this. Do not be disturbed by large numbers. Try to analyse the figures slowly to get a sense of the main features. In this case, the main feature is the dominance of consumer spending which amounts to about two-thirds of total spending. (You may have noticed that the figures for public spending in Table 2.4 and those of government spending in Table 2.5 are very different. That is because much of the public spending in the first table goes to others

TABLE 2.5 THE COMPONENTS OF AGGREGATE DEMAND 1998 (£ BILLION)

	£billion
Consumer expenditure	488
Government spending	145
Investment	142
Exports	242
Minus imports	–266
Total aggregate demand	751

Source: Adapted from *Economic Trends*, January, 2000, Table 2.2.

and is then spent in the shops. For example, most of the £102 billion social security budget goes to claimants and is spent by them, so it appears as part of the consumer expenditure component in Table 2.5.) Putting together spending on these items gives us the aggregate demand curve. The shape of this curve is similar to that of the demand curve we discussed earlier – it slopes down from left to right. There are several reasons for this, but we can summarise them by saying that, other things remaining equal, a rise in prices means that people will be poorer and so will buy fewer goods. And just as the microeconomic demand curve shifted, so will the aggregate demand curve. In this case, the factors that shift the curve include international factors and the government's fiscal and monetary policy. For example, an increase in foreign income will increase the demand for goods produced in the UK and shift the aggregate demand curve to the right. By fiscal policy we mean changes in tax and government spending. For instance, a rise in taxes will mean that people have less to spend, so the aggregate demand curve will move to the left as shown in Figure 2.10. At any particular price level, people will have less money and spend less so that national income will fall. A cut in taxes would have the opposite effect, it would raise national income.

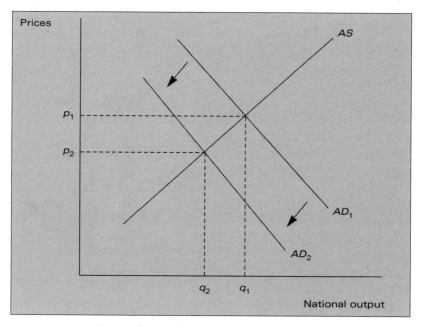

FIGURE 2.10   A FALL IN AGGREGATE DEMAND

Monetary policy is discussed later. Here we can say that if there is a cut in interest rates, some people will have more money to spend (for example, they will pay less on their mortgages) and so will have more money to spend on goods and services, causing the aggregate demand curve to shift to the right.

The shape of the aggregate supply curve is a matter of some controversy, and is discussed in detail in the next chapter. This curve shows the relationship between GDP (that is, national output) and the price level. For simplicity here we will say that it is made up by adding together the supply curves of individual firms. So, just as the supply curve of a particular firm slopes up to the right, so will the aggregate supply curve, showing that at higher prices, firms will be willing to supply more goods.

Just as there are shifts in an individual firm's supply curve, so there are shifts in the aggregate supply curve. For example, if there is an increase in productivity, more goods will be produced at every price level, as shown in Figure 2.11. Increases in productivity have several causes, such as increases in the quantity and quality of machinery, better management and better-educated workers. The supply curve would also shift to the right if there was a rise in the number of hours

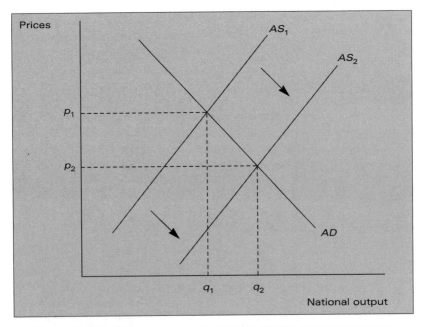

FIGURE 2.11 THE EFFECT OF A RISE IN THE NUMBER OF HOURS WORKED

worked. One of the reasons for the rise in living standards since the Second World War has been because more women have gone to work. This has shifted the *AS* curve to the right.

Let us now put the aggregate demand and aggregate supply curves together to show the effects of various changes. Figure 2.12 shows the effect of a shift to the right of the aggregate demand curve, for example, because the government has cut taxes or increased its spending. The same result would occur if there was a cut in interest rates, or if foreigners bought more of our goods.

As you can see, some of the consequences are very desirable. So far as output is concerned, the economy will produce more goods and services, and this probably means more jobs. But the effects are not entirely beneficial: prices rise. And as we will see in the next chapter, some economists argue that the increase in output will be very short-lived since the inflation will choke off expansion.

When the aggregate demand curve shifts to the left, the results are reversed. The consequences are lower prices, lower output and fewer jobs – the economy will move into a recession.

If shifts to the right in the aggregate demand curve are not entirely beneficial, shifts to the right in the aggregate supply curve are highly

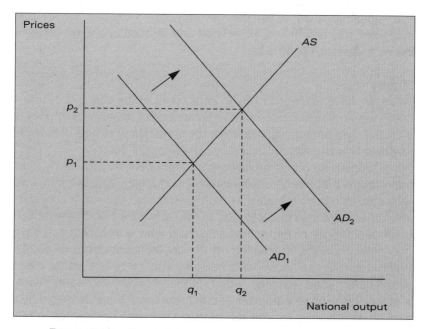

FIGURE 2.12   THE EFFECT OF AN INCREASE IN AGGREGATE DEMAND

desirable since they lead to lower prices and greater output, as was shown in Figure 2.11. Unfortunately these are difficult to obtain; you may remember that they are caused by such things as increases in productivity – easy to say, but difficult to obtain.

The implication of this analysis is that if governments want the economy to expand they should try to introduce measures that will increase productivity, for example, by improving education and training and by giving incentives for firms to invest. Similarly, the government can use its fiscal and monetary policy to shift the demand curve to ease the country out of recession, though this may cause inflation and the increase in output may not last for very long

These concepts of aggregate demand and aggregate supply can be used to develop policies for unemployment. If economic forecasters predict that the economy is going into recession, then if the government were to intervene by increasing its own spending and cutting taxes, the aggregate demand curve would shift to the right, increasing output and jobs.

Unfortunately, there are difficulties in this. Economic forecasters are not always right, and if the government increases aggregate demand to ward off a recession but no recession appears, the consequences will be very high inflation. Hence for some economists, the best policy to curb unemployment is for the government to use the supply-side measures, just mentioned. (This issue is discussed in greater detail in the next chapter, pp. 50–3.)

Money

So far we have managed to write an account of the contents of introductory economics courses with little mention of money. Yet, money is a crucial, and often misunderstood, phenomenon. It is best defined as anything that is generally accepted in payment of debt.

In a modern economy, money serves a number of functions. Its most important is that it acts as a medium of exchange. Without money we would have to rely on barter. As with most things, this has a considerable disadvantage in that it is easy to find someone who has what you want, but difficult to find the same person who wants what you have got! More formally, it depends on the double coincidence of wants. Without money, someone who has shoes to swap but wants bread would have to find someone with a surplus of bread who wants shoes.

Money also serves a number of other functions. For example, it acts as a store of value; we can put money aside and use it later to buy things that we want. One reason that inflation is undesirable is that it destroys this function. Money also acts as a unit of account and it allows the easy management of debts and loans.

For most of its history, money has required three characteristics: it had to be durable – money that melted is useless; it had to be scarce – sand could never serve as money in the Sahara, and it had to be divisible – elephants, which are scarce and durable, would not serve as money. Imagine going into a shop and asking for a box of matches whilst offering an elephant as payment. Gold and silver met these three requirements and were the basis of money for many years, but gradually became replaced by notes. For many years these were backed by gold, but this backing disappeared at the beginning of the twentieth century and now the Bank of England prints notes to meet the needs of the economy. That is because most money in a modern economy does not come in the form of notes or coins. Picture a typical worker's wages. Before these are paid into her bank account, her employer takes out tax and National Insurance. Then the money is transferred into the worker's bank account. Then money is taken out by direct debit or standing order to pay her mortgage and various insurances. In addition, when she buys things, she will often pay using a cheque or credit card. Now in all these transactions, not a note or coin has changed hands. The money that has changed hands depends not on its physical properties, but on the fact that it is accepted. That is why the European Union could introduce the euro in 1999 without the currency being backed by any real assets such as gold. Like other currencies, the euro has no intrinsic value; it is valuable only because it is accepted.

So if this money has no real physical existence, how does it come about? The answer is that it is created by the banking system. When a bank receives a deposit, it does not keep all the money until the depositor wishes to reclaim it; instead it keeps a proportion of the money and lends the rest. In turn, much of the money lent will be deposited in other banks which will only keep a proportion and lend the rest. When security is paramount, banks will keep a relatively high proportion of each deposit, but this is at the cost of profits since the more a bank lends, the higher will be its profits. What would be the effect of an unrestricted increase in the money supply? I have in my possession a German banknote for 10 million marks. Unfortunately, that does not make me rich since it was issued in 1923 when the German economy was in chaos, printing huge quantities of money and causing massive inflation –prices were more than doubling each day – so that money was not fulfilling any of its functions very well.

Now we have a very powerful theory about the relationship between the money supply and the rate of inflation: it is called the quantity theory of money. We can explain it best by using an equation:

$$MV = PQ$$

where M = the quantity of money
$\quad\quad\;\; V$ = the velocity of circulation
$\quad\quad\;\; P$ = the average price level in the economy
$\quad\quad\;\; Q$ = the quantity of goods produced in the economy

This equation is true by definition; it is really saying that what we spend – MV – equals what we buy – PQ.

A simplistic explanation of this theory may help you understand it. Imagine a small island where the total quantity of money (M) is 250 dollars; during any particular year each dollar is used four times (V), so that total spending is $250 \times 4 = 1000$. Now assume that in this economy 500 items (Q) are produced each year. Hence we can conclude that that the average price (P) of each item is 2 dollars, that is:

$$MV = PQ$$
$$250 \times 4 = 2 \times 500$$

But what happens if the quantity of money rises from 250 to 500 dollars whilst the velocity and the quantity of goods remain the same? That is:

$$500 \times 4 = ? \times 500$$

The answer is that prices rise from 2 dollars to 4 dollars.

The real world is obviously much more complex than this, but if we make some assumptions, such as that the velocity of circulation is constant, then we can conclude that changes in the money supply will lead to price rises. And if we want to stop inflation, the policy is clear: control the money supply.

This is a theory that has had profound effects. The Bank of England in the UK and the European Central Bank in euro countries are charged with keeping down inflation. The method they use to do this is to control the money supply. It should be pointed out that this policy is not universally accepted. Some economists argue that this policy results in lower output and higher unemployment. An alternative method is for the government to cut back aggregate demand by putting up taxes and cutting its own spending. This will shift the aggregate demand curve to the left, leading to lower prices, but also to lower output and higher inflation. So no policy to control inflation is painless.

International trade

Most introductory economics courses follow the pattern we have done here and end with a section on international aspects. This does not mean that this is unimportant. We live in a world where what happens in one country has profound effects on others. For example, a recession in one large country will spill over and affect all those who trade with it, causing recessions there.

We want to look here at the advantages and disadvantages of international trade, a subject of much ignorance among non-economists. Many people would suggest that exports are good because they bring money into the country and create jobs here whilst imports are bad because they have the opposite effect.

This is economic nonsense. The first economist to point this out was Adam Smith in *The Wealth of Nations,* which he wrote in 1776. In this book, he made use of the idea of specialisation, one of the aspects of the 'How to produce?' question. He wrote

> It is the maxim of every prudent master of a family never to attempt to make at home what it will cost him more to make than to buy. The tailor does not attempt to make his own shoes, but buys them off the shoemaker. The shoemaker does not attempt to make his own clothes, but buys them off the tailor . . . What is prudence in the conduct of a private family can scarce be folly in the conduct of a great kingdom . . . If a foreign country can supply us with a commodity cheaper than we ourselves can make it, better buy it off them with some part of the produce of our own country.

To give an extreme example of this idea, it would be quite possible for Britain to grow tropical produce, but this would require huge quantities of energy and be very expensive. Far better for Britain to buy such goods from tropical countries and to pay for this by exporting goods we can make relatively efficiently. The central concept here is that of opportunity cost. The opportunity cost of growing tropical fruit would be very high.

Adam Smith's ideas on trade were taken up and developed by another great economist called David Ricardo in 1817, and it is his ideas which form the basis of current thinking by economists on international trade. Adam Smith's idea has been called '*absolute advantage*' – that countries should trade when they are absolutely better than another in producing a good, just as the tailor is absolutely better than the shoemaker at making clothes. But what about the position when a country is *relatively* better at producing many goods than another?

The easiest way to explain this rather complex notion is to do what Smith did and consider individuals rather than countries. Imagine two people, A and B. A is a hundred times better than B at brain surgery and ten times better than B at road-sweeping. Now what is the most efficient way for A and B to allocate their time? One answer is that since A is better than B at both jobs, she should do both jobs, spending some time at surgery and some at road-sweeping. B would do the same. But this would be inefficient since she would be spending time at jobs where she was only ten times as efficient when she could be working at jobs where she was a hundred times as efficient. Similarly B would be spending time at a job where she was a hundred times less efficient than A. Far better for A to spend all her time on surgery and B to spend all her time road-sweeping.

Ricardo developed his idea by using the example of Britain and Portugal. He suggested that Portugal was more efficient at producing both wine and cloth, but concluded that for Portugal 'it would be . . . advantageous for her to export wine in exchange for cloth . . . she would obtain more cloth from England than she could produce by diverting a portion of her capital from the cultivation of vines to the manufacture of cloth'.

The implications of Ricardo's theories are enormous. A country which is efficient in producing many goods should not try to produce them all, but should concentrate on those areas where it is *relatively* more efficient. These goods can then be sold to buy goods from other countries. In this way output is maximised.

Of course, the idea as presented here has been oversimplified. For example, it has ignored transport costs and also the prices at which the goods are sold. But its conclusion is clear: countries should specialise and exchange, just as individuals do.

There are other advantages from international trade. An obvious one is that trade produces choice. If we could only buy goods made in our own country, we would be deprived of the huge variety of goods that come from other countries. Producing for overseas markets also gives rise to the advantages of large-scale production, which means lower costs to pass on to consumers. Moreover, trade also creates competition. When imports are restricted, domestic producers have a secure market. They have little need to improve their efficiency and they can push up prices with impunity so that consumers have less choice and pay higher prices. Restrictions on trade tend to benefit a few producers – which is why they complain so often about foreign competition – but the people who lose out from such restrictions are the mass of consumers who are usually less vocal about what they are missing.

Of course, there are arguments to be made about the disadvantages of foreign trade. One of these concerns dumping. This occurs when a firm sells its product overseas at less than the cost of production. It might do this, for example, in the hope of destroying competitors so that it could take over their markets and subsequently raise prices. However, many complaints about dumping are not justified. When a firm expands output, its marginal cost may be very low; this means that it could sell abroad this extra production at a very low price, so benefiting foreign consumers.

Similarly, some firms complain about having to compete with foreign firms that can pay lower wages. In addition to the economic arguments against restricting such competition, there are moral ones: such a policy would mean that workers in very poor countries would lose their jobs and become even poorer.

A stronger argument in favour of restricting trade is called the infant industry argument. This suggests that in some cases, a new industry, often in a developing country, cannot compete with established firms overseas who have the advantage of experience, but that given a few years' protection, the infant industry would grow up and become as efficient. There is some merit in this argument, but all too often such protected industries never do grow up and become a permanent source of inefficiency and misallocation of resources.

So far as international trade is concerned, most economists would argue that most restrictions on trade diminish economic welfare. Let both imports and exports flourish!

▶ Options in economics courses

So far, we have outlined the main concepts and ideas that you are likely to meet in an introductory courses in economics. But that is not the whole story, since almost all economics courses offer options which either run alongside introductions to the subject or which develop ideas which have been dealt with only briefly.

It is not possible to describe these, since they usually reflect the academic interests of the lecturers. Typical options might include development economics, international economics, and industrial and business economics. Courses in social economics and the history of economic ideas are also common. Most degree courses in economics will include a course on mathematics and statistics. Usually, this is an introductory course which students with GCSE mathematics can be expected to pass. Chapter 5 in this book outlines the main features of such a course. Many universities will also offer the option to take more advanced courses in mathematical economics.

In choosing your options it is best to bear in mind three criteria: your interests, your other courses and your future career. You will usually get better results if you choose options that interest you. So if you have a particular interest in, say, the social aspects of economics, then choose those courses that reflect this aspect of the subject. If the financial courses appeal, then choose those. Sometimes it is possible to take economics courses that fit with your other studies. For example, an option in business economics would be an obvious choice for someone whose other courses are business studies or accounting. The other criterion is your future career. If you want a job in financial services, then it is obviously appropriate to choose options that are relevant.

▶ Conclusion

We have tried in this chapter to focus on the main economic concepts and theories which you are likely to find in an introductory course in economics. It is not possible in one chapter to cover an entire course, but if you have understood the main points here, you will have a solid foundation on which to build.

In order to give you this foundation we have focused on a few core concepts. These include opportunity cost, demand, supply, and various cost and revenue concepts in microeconomics. In macroeconomics we have used the concepts of aggregate demand and aggregate supply to study how the economy operates and have examined the quantity theory of money and the advantages in international trade.

If you understand these concepts they will stand you in good stead in all your economics courses.

Reference and further reading

Smith, A. (1776) *The Wealth of Nations*, available in many editions.

You will probably have a course text suggested to you by tutors. Sometimes these will be very large texts. These can confuse since they go into considerable detail, but they are often essential to develop your understanding. Hence, it is sometimes a good idea to have access to shorter books that often focus on the main points.

3 Mainstream Approaches to Economics

▶ Neo-classical economics

Economic theories do not just appear in a void. They grow out of foundations laid in the past and reflect changing economic circumstances. Adam Smith, whom we met in Chapter 2 is often called the 'father' of economics. His great book *The Wealth of Nations* was written in 1776 at a time when Britain was experiencing the first industrial revolution. Although the country was still largely agricultural, new industries were developing, international trade was growing and there was a movement of people from village to town. These developments stimulated Smith and despite the passage of time, many of the ideas he developed then still have great relevance. For example, we have already discussed his view that international trade was beneficial. This idea was linked to another: that there were great advantages to be obtained if workers specialised – if there was extensive division of labour. In a famous passage he analysed a nail factory where one person was responsible for heating the metal, another for drawing out the wire, another for cutting it and so on. In this way a small group of workers could produce thousands of nails a day, far more than if numbers of workers attempted to do all the work themselves. The main reason for this high productivity was that when people specialised at a job they became experts at it. However, specialisation requires a large market – and this is one of the benefits of trade.

Perhaps Smith's biggest contribution was his argument that markets were the best way to allocate resources. This was his answer to our three big questions posed in Chapter 2. He argued that 'it is not from the benevolence of the butcher, the brewer or the baker that we expect our dinner but from their regard to their own self interest' (Smith, 1776, p. 119). So, in a market economy, workers seek higher wages, whilst owners want to pay low wages and charge high prices whilst consumers want low prices. These seemingly conflicting pressures are resolved in a market as if there were an 'invisible hand' coordinating the process. Competition would bring prices down and force inefficient firms out of business so that consumers would benefit. Moreover, the system had built-in incentives so that, for example, workers would move to expanding industries where wages were rising. The result would be to maximise economic welfare.

The overall implication of Smith's analysis was that markets could usually look after themselves with little intervention from government. However, he did recognise that there were very important responsibilities for government, for example, in combating monopoly because 'the price of monopoly is on every occasion the highest which can be got' (p. 164). Monopoly occurred because 'People of the same trade seldom meet together, even for merriment or diversion, but the conversation ends in a conspiracy against the public in some contrivance to raise prices' (p. 232). Hence, government needed to intervene to prevent these unsatisfactory results of individuals seeking to maximise their own benefits.

Smith's contribution did not end there; he also discussed the factors that determined wages, rents and prices and commented on the functions of money in an economy.

Later economists built on these foundations which were so solid that they became known as 'classical'. Just over a hundred years after Smith, another great economist called Alfred Marshall gave us the theoretical apparatus which is still used. He developed the ideas of Smith and other economists, so he is sometimes called a neo-classical economist ('neo' meaning new).

Marshall defined economics as the study of man 'in the ordinary business of life'. His ideas were put forward in his great book *Principles of Economics* which was published in 1890. He argued that economics was not 'a body of concrete truth, but an engine for the discovery of concrete truth' (quoted in Barber, 1967, p. 169).

For Marshall, as for other neo-classical economists, the big question was 'What determined prices?' This meant that they tended to neglect other questions such as the determinants of economic growth, but their work on price gave us the approach that is still used by economists. The analysis of demand and supply described in the first chapter is really that of Alfred Marshall. He developed these two concepts and introduced the demand-and-supply diagrams that are so familiar to all economists. He likened these curves to the twin blades of a pair of scissors. Both blades were needed if the scissors were to do their job, and both demand and supply were needed if we were to discover the factors which determined price.

It is neither possible nor desirable to write a history of economic thought here. What we have tried to do is to give a flavour of the work of two giants on which most modern economic analysis rests. As we will see in the next chapter, radical economists reject some of these neo-classical approaches, and indeed discuss other aspects of the economy. But neo-classical economics remains the foundation.

▶ Modern developments

Mainstream economics can be roughly divided between three groups which for simplicity we can call neo-classical (or supply-side) Keynesian – this called after another great British economist called John Maynard Keynes – and Austrian. It would be wrong, however, to imagine that there are three completely separate groups of economists; there is considerable overlap between the groups, and they often adapt each other's ideas.

Modern neo-classical economists tend to be strong supporters of the use of markets to allocate resources. Whilst they accept that government needs to intervene to prevent monopoly and to provide services such as defence and law and order, they are sceptical about the need for other interventions. For example, one of their leaders, an American Nobel Prize winner called Milton Friedman quotes with approval Smith's account of duties of the government:

> first the duty of protecting the society from the violence and invasion of other violent societies; secondly, the duty of protecting, as far as possible, every member of society from the injustice or oppression of every other member of it . . . ; and, thirdly, the duty of erecting and maintaining certain public works and public institutions. (1980, p. 48)

The essential assumption behind Friedman's approach is that individual adults are competent to make their own decisions: 'We believe in freedom except for madmen or children' (p. 53). In other words, people should be regarded as being responsible for the consequences of their own decisions; no government intervention is needed except to protect those who are unable to help themselves.

This assumption of competence may seem reasonable – after all, we are capable, aren't we? – but the consequences are profound. There is little need for a government to provide a health service, because people are capable of making their own arrangements, for example through private insurance. Similarly, there is little need for state old age pensions or for unemployment benefit or most other social security benefits since competent individuals should not rely on the state. This means that many taxes, particularly income tax, could be reduced or even abolished. Although not all neo-classical economists would agree with these specific proposals, they all look with favour on proposals to reduce the impact of government on the economy.

In macroeconomics, the emphasis of this group of economists is on controlling inflation. They believe that inflation distorts the economy since money cannot fulfil its functions and they emphasise control of the money supply as suggested earlier. As Milton Friedman (1980, p. 316) put it, 'Just as an excessive increase in the quantity of money is the one and only important cause of inflation, so a reduction in the rate of monetary growth is the one and only cure for inflation.' For this reason, these economists are sometimes called 'monetarists'.

Their attitude to unemployment is a little more difficult to explain. In the last chapter we drew the aggregate supply curve at roughly a 45-degree angle. For these economists, that is only true in the very short run. In the longer term, the aggregate supply curve is vertical. That is because they argue that the economy is normally in equilibrium at the full-employment level of output. If the government tries to stimulate the economy, then firms will have to attract more labour. They can only do this by paying higher wages. In turn, this will push up prices so that the real wage falls. (The real wage is the money wage adjusted to take account of inflation. If money wages rise by 5 per cent and prices also rise by 5 per cent, then the real wage is unchanged.) This fall in the real wage means that those people who were attracted into employment by the higher wages will realise that their wage has fallen; hence they will drift out of the labour market. This fall in the labour supply will mean that the only result of the government's policy is a rise in prices; there is no permanent increase in unemployment.

This process is illustrated in Figure 3.1. The economy is in equilibrium at point a where AD_1 intersects with AS – this is the short-run aggregate supply curve. If the government stimulates the economy, for example by cutting taxes or increasing its spending, the result will be a movement to b: an increase in output (and hence employment) and a rise in prices and money wages. However, for these economists, this is only temporary. The rise in prices will cut real wages, people will leave the labour market and output will fall back to a. This is the long-run equilibrium position. The result of the government's action is that there is no increase in output, just a rise in prices. Hence the long run aggregate supply curve is a vertical line through ac. This is the full-employment level of output.

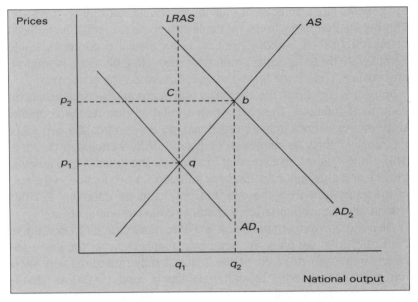

FIGURE 3.1   LONG-RUN AGGREGATE SUPPLY

At the heart of this argument is *time*. How quickly does the economy – and the labour market in particular – adjust to changes in real wages? Many supply-side economists argue that adjustment takes place very quickly: workers change jobs and move in and out of the labour market very freely. If this is true, then there is no point in the government attempting to stimulate the economy by increasing aggregate demand. The result would just be inflation.

Other economists dispute this. Keynes once said, 'In the long run we are all dead', meaning that unemployment would persist if appropriate policies were not adopted. Even if they are, Keynesians tend to argue that economies take a long time to adjust. This implies that the increase in output arising from a shift in the aggregate demand curve might last for a long time and so be a worthwhile policy to adopt.

The other implication of this analysis so far as these neo-classical economists are concerned is that unemployment can be regarded as voluntary because the economy is in equilibrium. In microeconomics, at the equilibrium price, the market clears so that firms can sell all they are willing to produce at this price. Similarly, at the macro level, the labour market clears, meaning that all those who are willing to work at the going wage rate can find jobs. If they are unemployed and want work, then the remedy is in their own hands: they must be willing to work at lower wages. As people lower the wage that they are willing to work for, at some point they will be able to find an employer willing to employ them.

We have mentioned the Keynesian belief that the economy only adjusts slowly. The other big disagreement between Keynesians and neo-classical economists is the belief of Keynesians that the economy can be in equilibrium at less than the full-employment level of output. In other words, for Keynesians the equilibrium shown in Figure 3.1 at output q_1 may be at a level of output at which many workers who want jobs cannot find work. Government action to increase aggregate demand can raise output and employment, though this will mean higher prices; it may be worthwhile if the unpleasant effects of inflation are less than the unpleasant effects of unemployment.

Our third group of economists are called 'Austrian' – though you don't have to be an Austrian citizen to be an Austrian economist. The name arose because of the work of an Austrian economist called Carl Menger who published a book called *Principles of Economics* in 1871 (Boettke, 1994). Menger's ideas attracted much support among other Austrian economists before their influence spread to other countries, hence the name 'Austrian'. They have many similarities with neo-classical economists; rather less with Keynesians.

Austrian methodology has three main features. The first is individualism. By this I mean they concentrate on the actions of individuals rather than groups. This means that they study national economies by looking at the actions of individual people. So, for these economists, if we want to discover what causes economies to grow, we do not start by looking at aggregates such as aggregate demand; instead we look at what motivates individual people to produce more goods. This is in complete contrast to Keynes's emphasis on macroeconomics.

The second feature of Austrian methodology is called subjectivism. This is difficult to explain, but essentially it recognises that people think. So if Mrs Smith thinks something is a good buy, then it is a good buy, even if it is more expensive than a similar product. Similarly, on the cost side, if Mr Jones thinks that income taxes are too high, making it not worthwhile to work, then taxes *are* too high. In other words, the individual's perceptions of costs, such as opportunity cost, are what matter. For these economists, the individual's active, inquiring mind is the beginning of economics. This means that they are sceptical about objective economic phenomena, and consequently they are usually not associated with mathematical economics. Instead, it is more philosophical than most other economics.

The third methodological aspect is that where neo-classical economists focus on equilibrium, Austrians pay attention to processes rather than equilibrium states since markets may never reach equilibrium. Hence they argue that we should pay more attention to how markets change than where they end up.

These three methodological features have considerable implications for particular aspects of economics. Let us look at competition as an example. For Austrian economists, competition has nothing to do with market structures such as perfect competition and monopoly. They argue that it is inconceivable that any monopolist has no competition at all which influences its activities. Neo-classical economists argue that barriers to entry in an industry are undesirable since they reduce competition and allow firms to make excess profits. For Austrians, it is in the nature of rivalry between firms that entrepreneurs erect barriers to ensure their own success and to compete. Competition means preventing others from being successful. Hence barriers to entry are an essential feature of the competitive process.

One consequence of this approach is that Austrians give much attention to the role of the entrepreneur. Mainstream economists tend to assume that the mere existence of possibilities of profit is sufficient to ensure their exploitation. Austrians disagree; they argue that we need to examine the subjective opinions of individual entrepreneurs. Thus a great Austrian economist called Schumpeter analysed competition by studying the role of the entrepreneur. Schumpeter introduced the idea of 'creative destruction'. This suggests that economies develop – and monopolies collapse – when entrepreneurs take risks and introduce new techniques or products. For example, the old monopoly of the canals was destroyed by the arrival of railways, the power of a few manufacturers of typewriters was destroyed by the creation of computers, and the arrival of mobile telephones has destroyed the monopoly of land-based telephone systems.

The methodological concern with process rather than with conclusions means that Austrians are sceptical about demand-and-supply analysis. When demand rises, most economists would say that this leads to a price rise. Austrians would be reluctant to accept this. For these economists, when price rises, entrepreneurs in the retail trade will place orders for more goods. This will usually lead to more resources being devoted to producing the good. If this can be done without an increase in the price of the resource, then more goods will be produced without any price rise. Hence, Austrians focus on what happens when there is a change, such as an increase in demand. They do not assume that this will lead to equilibrium. Instead there may be shortages and no equilibrium. This does not mean that they reject supply and demand as concepts, but that they merely use these concepts as part of their overall analysis.

One final point about the Austrians. They tend to dislike government intervention in the economy such as regulation because they believe that this leads to more problems – entrepreneurs spend more time responding to regulations than producing better products. Hence they are fiercely critical of economic planning. This means that they also dislike the idea of nationalised industries in particular and 'socialist' ideas in general.

▶ How economists work

Economists want to understand how economies work – to find the best solutions to the three questions 'What', 'How', 'Who'. One reason for this is the simple joy of finding out. If this were not a powerful force for humans we would be back in the Stone Age. But for most economists, the pleasure of understanding is accompanied by a desire to provide solutions for problems faced by human societies. And better economies can mean better quality of life. So the work of economists is important, and, indeed, the higher living standards which millions of people have compared to those of our ancestors are in large part the result of economists making good policy prescriptions.

The first step in the work of an economist is descriptive: 'What is happening in the economic world?' This involves observing and measuring various aspects of economic activity. Fortunately, much of this work is now done by governments and various other groups who publish statistics on economic activity. Sometimes, however, obtaining data requires much detailed activity. Thus, governments publish a great deal of data on unemployment, but sometimes this will be augmented by individual economists investigating the consequences for various groups. For example, finding out what happens to the incomes of young workers when they lose their jobs would require specific investigation since this information is not available from official statistics. The sources of much information are given in Chapter 9.

Description is not enough. If we want to understand what is happening in the economic world, we have to build models to show how the economy operates. A model is really a simplification of reality. There are potentially millions and millions of pieces of economic information. The price of a haircut, the number of corn flakes packets bought in a particular shop, the money earned by a paper-boy – these are all part of the economic world. So the first job of the economist is to sort out what is important in a particular context, just as we would focus on the essentials if someone asked us the way to the station. In this case we would omit descriptions of the lamp-posts, litter bins and house curtains and concentrate on the main roads. Similarly, economists building models concentrate on what they think are the essential features.

So, an economic model is a simplified version of the real world, focusing on the elements that seem relevant. For example, a model of the determinants of saving might include such things as the level of income, the rate of interest and the amount of savings done in the past. Similarly, when we wrote $AD = C + I + G + X - M$ (p. 34), we were developing a model of the determinants of aggregate demand, just as we did when writing an equation for the factors that influenced demand for individual goods.

Economic models can come in many different forms. In some cases, they will be in the form of one or more equations. In others, they will be presented diagrammatically or verbally.

An economic theory is developed by building and testing models; sometimes models are shown to be inadequate, just as directions on how to get to the station may be inadequate. So, economists begin by building a model. Since the real world is so complicated, this often involves making assumptions. We had an example of this in developing our model of demand when we assumed *ceteris paribus* – that everything remained the same except for one variable such as income. The model is then used to generate predictions. In the case of income, we predicted that an increase in income would lead to a rise in demand. Much empirical investigation has shown that this is generally true – but not always. For some goods, such as light bulbs and salt, a rise in income has little or no effect on demand. Hence we need to modify and qualify our theory.

Economic models have three elements: at least one variable whose behaviour is to be explained – in the case that we have just discussed, this is demand; at least one variable that provides an explanation – in this case, income; and behavioural assumptions that explain how the dependent variable is related to the independent variable – in this case that a rise in one (income) leads to a rise in the other (demand).

Economics as a science
So, does this methodology make economics a science?

The answer to this question depends on how we define 'science'. Since there are many definitions of 'science' it is probable that economics will fit some of these but not others.

One objection to categorising economics as a science is that science is sometimes associated with the development of universal laws such as Newton's universal law of gravity. This is not possible with economics, since our subject is concerned with the behaviour of humans, and human behaviour differs over time and place. For example, at one time almost all men and women wore hats or caps when outside the home. This is now very rare, but this change would have been very difficult to predict if we were trying to develop a model of the demand for hats. Similarly, the optimism or pessimism of entrepreneurs will influence whether or not they invest in new machinery. Optimism varies over time, is not always rational and so is difficult to forecast.

Another objection to classifying economics as a science is that it is not possible to conduct experiments, something which is strongly associated with most sciences. Although this objection is not quite true – there have been a very few experiments investigating such things as human spending, it is largely true that in all the social sciences, experimentation is difficult or impossible for ethical reasons. It is also impossible because of the complexity of human economic life – imagine trying to conduct an experiment to see if an increase in government spending led to a fall in unemployment. This would be impossible because so many other factors would be changing at the same time, making it impossible to tease out cause and effect. However, experiments are not essential for classification as a science – astronomy, for example, is a science, yet astronomers' opportunities to experiment are limited: for example, they cannot switch off the sun to see what happens.

A final objection to calling economics a science is that it is inexact. Economists can never develop the precise formulae of disciplines such as physics. Yet other sciences such as biology are often inexact, and what seems exact, such as Newton's law of gravity, is sometimes subsequently discovered to fall short of the whole truth (in this case by Einstein).

The strongest factor in the claim of economics to be called a science is its methodology; if the methods used by economists follow the pattern of those used by other sciences, then economics can realistically be called a science.

This is not the place to develop a treatise on the methodology of science, so we will content ourselves by looking at the work of two philosophers of science, Popper (1959) and Kuhn (1970).

Sir Karl Popper was born in Austria at the beginning of the twentieth century, but later moved to the UK where he taught at the London School of Economics. In Popper's view, science is a matter of imaginative conjecture to which is added 'falsification'. By falsification Popper means that a theory proves its strength by withstanding our attempts to refute it. It is the capacity for being falsified that distinguishes science from non-science. For example, we have seen that Milton Friedman has argued that inflation is always caused by an increase in the money supply. This is falsifiable – for example, if we found an example of inflation which was not caused by an increase in the money supply. (Of course, in practice, falsification may be difficult. In this example, money supply and prices may both rise, but it is difficult to show which causes which.) So, if we accept Popper's definition of scientific method, then economics is a science.

Kuhn takes a different approach. He points out that scientific knowledge tends to develop in fits and starts – periods of great progress are followed by years of stagnation. He explains this by arguing that groups of people with a particular viewpoint, which he calls 'colleges', come together and tend to dominate a subject. For many years, this can be accepted as true and not questioned – the view that the sun revolves round the earth is an example of this. During this time, there is little scientific progress. However, evidence gradually develops which contradicts this dominant view. It is then successfully challenged and a new dominant view is established. If Kuhn's argument is accepted, then economics also (probably) counts as a science. The dominant approach for many years has been the neo-classical one, built on the work of Marshall. Keynes challenged this; in turn, Keynesian economics was attacked by reinvigorated groups of neo-classical economists. These are also challenged by other economists whose approaches have not been accepted into the dominant paradigm, but which are certainly challenging. Some of these are discussed in the next chapter.

Common fallacies

There are three common errors or fallacies which are common in economics; in your reading you should be on the lookout for these.

The first is really a product of wishful thinking: economists investigating a problem want to find some result. Given the huge amount of possible data that might be relevant in most investigations, there is a possibility that something will turn up which appears to show a relationship between variables. An example will make this clearer. Suppose you are investigating the relationship between two variables such as poor health and unemployment. Now, there are many ways of measuring both these variables. Poor health could be measured by examining data such as hospital admissions, attendance at doctors' surgeries or as a result of questionnaires asking people about their health. Similarly, there are various ways of measuring unemployment. If many statistics about these two variables are put into a computer, it is quite possible that the statistical analysis will show some statistical relationship. Now, this may be true – indeed, we have chosen this example because we think that there is evidence to support the hypothesis that poor health is an important consequence of unemployment – unemployed people often feel depressed and this then leads to other ailments. But it is also possible that a statistical relationship may be the result of chance, or indeed, that causation is the other way round – that bad health is likely to cause unemployment. The problems that can arise in using data are discussed in more detail in Chapter 9.

A second common fallacy is that of composition. It seems obvious that what is true of the part is true of the whole. But this is not so, particularly in macroeconomics. Thus if one firm cuts its labour force, it may increase its profits. However, if all firms do this, the result will be a fall in incomes in the economy as a whole. This will then lead to a fall in sales and lower profits. So what is true of a part may not apply to the whole.

The Romans named our third fallacy and it is still very common – if you listen to politicians you will hear it very frequently. The Roman expression for it was *post hoc ergo propter hoc*, which translated means 'after this, therefore because of this'. A simple example will show that when one event follows another, the first event does not necessarily cause the second event. If I water my garden and then it rains, then, clearly, my watering has not caused it to rain. Similarly, if a man buys a wedding ring for his girlfriend, this is not the cause of the subsequent marriage. Rather the reverse – it is the decision to marry that causes the man to buy the ring.

In economics it is often difficult to distinguish cause and effect, so this *post hoc* fallacy is very common. If a government increases the quantity of money and this is followed by a rise in prices, has the increase in money supply caused the inflation? It is certainly quite possible, but it is also possible that the rise in money supply was the result of earlier inflation, or that some other event caused the inflation. Similarly, if there is a rise in share prices and an economic boom follows this, has the rise in share prices caused the boom? It is certainly possible, but it is also possible that some other event, such as a boom in other countries, has caused both events to happen.

Disagreement among economists

There is a well-known joke amongst economists to the effect that if all the economists in the world were laid end to end they would not reach a conclusion. As often happens, the joke contains an element of truth; economists often do argue about their subject. But this is no bad thing since, as we have seen, disagreement can lead to progress. If everyone always agreed that the earth was flat, the truth would never be discovered. So, economics is not unusual: there is disagreement in all scientific subjects.

There are several reasons for this so far as economics is concerned. The main reason is that people are complicated: it is impossible to predict their behaviour. One way to overcome this difficulty is the law of large numbers. This suggests that although we cannot predict the actions of any particular person, we can make good predictions about large numbers. Thus we cannot say whether Mr X will watch Manchester United's next match, but we can make fairly good predictions that, if Manchester United is at home to another large club, then the ground will be full.

However, this does not solve all the difficulties. Over time, large numbers of people do change their economic actions. Thus when the BSE beef scare occurred, thousands of people stopped eating beef. This was not predictable in advance. Moreover, sometimes the evidence is not 'hard', that is, accurate. For example, data about people's incomes are difficult to obtain since these are usually collected by the income tax authorities and many people lie about their incomes when completing tax forms. So, disagreements often arise when the available evidence is not sufficiently strong for a clear conclusion to be reached.

But there is another reason why economists disagree. That is because their values differ. For example, the most common way for economists to measure the performance of an economy is to use statistics for GDP. However, a growing number of economists reject this approach, saying that GDP statistics do not represent welfare. If we build miles of roads, then the money spent on this will show up as a rise in GDP, but welfare might actually be less since the roads may have led to a decline in environmental assets. So people's values, in this case about the value of the environment, can affect economic analysis. They can also affect the actual statistics. How do we decide how many people are poor? Or how many have inadequate housing? The answer to these questions will often depend on the individual since there is no completely objective way of deciding such questions.

Similarly, policy prescriptions given by economists often reflect their personal opinions as much as their objective analysis. An economist employed by big business could easily develop a persuasive argument to show that it would be beneficial economically if trade union power was curtailed; one working for the unions might come to a very different conclusion. One of the benefits of studying economics is that it makes it possible for you to come to your own reasoned conclusions.

In part, these disagreements reflect a distinction between two aspects of economics. *Positive* economics is concerned with what is, was or will be. Positive statements are usually testable, at least in principle, though that might not be possible in practice, for example because relevant statistics may not be available. When they are testable, they can be refuted – remember Popper's criterion for science?

Examples of positive statements which might or might not be true:

- People save more as incomes rise
- An increase in the price of mobile phones will cause people to buy more of them
- On average economists are taller than accountants
- A rise in income tax will cause people to work less

These positive statements can be contrasted with *normative* ones. Normative statements depend on value judgements: they are concerned with what *ought* to be and their truth cannot be determined by reference to the facts.

Examples of normative statements:

- Unemployment is a more serious problem than inflation
- Economists are better-looking than accountants
- Britain is a better country now than it was ten years ago

This difference between positive and normative economics is one reason why economists disagree. In other words, they are disagreeing about normative statements, not about positive ones.

One final point about disagreements between economists. Public arguments conceal a real truth: *economists often agree with each other!* For example, most economists would agree about the benefits of free trade, though they might differ on particular aspects. They would also agree about the benefits that the use of markets to allocate resources could bring. They would also agree that price controls tend to lead to shortages. These are just three examples of substantial agreement between economists, so do not be misled by talk of disagreement to imagine that this is the full story.

▶ Conclusion

Modern economics has built on the work of the classical economists such as Smith and Marshall. The ideas which they developed, such as demand-and-supply analysis, are at the heart of the work of most modern economists, though it is possible to divide many current practitioners into three main groups: the neo-classicists, the Keynesians and the Austrians. This distinction is rather crude since there are many overlaps and borrowings between these groups. For simplicity, and rather crudely, we can say that Keynesians tend to focus on the demand side of the economy and to be concerned with the short run. Neo-classicists focus on the long run and on the supply side of the economy whilst Austrians focus on the individual and tend to be dismissive of concepts relating to the economy as a whole such as aggregate demand. All three groups employ 'scientific' methods, such as building and testing models, and make use of Popper's criterion – by trying to falsify theories.

We also looked at disagreements among economists. In part these arise because the real world is so complex and because data are not always available to test out theories. But disagreements also arise because economists – like all people – have different values and these affect their work. However, many disagreements are about normative economics and indeed there is substantial agreement among most economists.

References

Boettke, P. J. (ed.) (1994) *The Elgar Companion to Austrian Economics*, Aldershot, Edward Elgar.

Kuhn, T. (1970) *The Structure of Scientific Revolutions*, University of Chicago Press.

Popper, K. (1959) *The Logic of Scientific Discovery*, New York, Harper.

Smith, A. (1776) *The Wealth of Nations,* reprinted in Penguin Classics, 1986.

Further reading

Barber, W. J. (1967) *A History of Economic Ideas*, Harmondsworth, Penguin.

Friedman, R. and Friedman, M. (1980) *Free to Choose*, Harmondsworth, Penguin.

4 Competing Approaches in Economics

In the last chapter we looked at the way in which most economists approach their work, and we looked at three approaches in particular. These were the neo-classical, which is the dominant approach in modern economics, the Keynesian and the Austrian. These can all be regarded as 'mainstream', though no doubt some economists would disagree.

In this chapter we want to look at more radical approaches to the subject and we will consider three of these. One of them, the Marxian, is long-standing, but has not managed to become dominant. The other two, which we will call environmental and feminist, are more recent. We will begin by looking at the Marxian approach, which has the most developed theoretical underpinning.

▶ The Marxian approach to economics

First, a word about words. This section is headed 'Marxian'. This is the word used to describe those social scientists who make considerable use of Marx's ideas, but who realise that it is a long time since he wrote – and he was not infallible – so his ideas have to be adapted to take account of historical changes. This contrasts with 'Marxists' who tend to view his works rather as Christians approach the bible, that is, as ultimate truth.

Marx's works are often judged, particularly by those who have not read him, as having been tried and found to fail in countries such as the former Soviet Union. Marxians would dispute this. They would argue that Marxian ideas were never implemented in the USSR and its allies, just as Christians would argue that Christ's ideas have never been implemented in 'Christian' countries. Marx must be judged on his ideas.

As its name implies, Marxian economics derives largely from the work of one man, Karl Marx, though others have contributed, most notably Friedrich Engels with whom Marx wrote the revolutionary pamphlet *The Communist Manifesto* in 1848. Marx was born in Germany in 1818 and died in 1893 – the year in which Keynes was born. Consequently, his writing was heavily influenced by the rapid spread of industrialisation which came to dominate European economies during his lifetime.

Marxians would generally agree that Marx gives a framework for analysis which should be varied according to time and place. At the time of the Russian revolution in 1917, Lenin adopted Marx's ideas and applied them to a country that had not yet achieved capitalist development. Later, in China, Mao attempted to use Marx's framework in terms of a much more backward rural economy. Contemporary Marxians, such as Cuba's Fidel Castro, take Marx's analysis and apply its ideas to the world economy at the beginning of a new millennium.

When he was 17, Marx went to university in Bonn to study law. Whilst there he took an active part in the social life of the community and was once arrested for drunkenness. Later, he married and had five children, though three of these died whilst Marx was still alive. His political views made him unpopular with the authorities, and he was forced to leave Germany. Eventually, he settled in Britain where he spent the last part of his life. He continued to be active in left-wing politics, but spent most of his time researching in the British Museum and writing, most notably the three volumes of *Capital* that he wrote over a long period starting in the 1860s. Marx only saw the first volume published in his own lifetime; Engels edited the other two from Marx's notes. His underlying methodology is to be found in his *Critique of Political Value; Capital* uses this method to develop a critique of capitalism.

Marxian economics is often ignored in economics courses, partly because it is difficult to understand. There are several reasons for this. One is that much of this writing was produced from his notes and reflects the concerns of his own time, which may not be ours. Moreover, his theory involves a lot of abstract theorising and use of concepts not found in conventional economics. Finally, Marx was not just an economist; rather his economics forms part of a wider philosophical approach. Indeed, he was first and foremost a philosopher who was not able to formulate his theory until he had mastered economics.

This wider approach meant that his major concern was not with such things as the allocation of scarce resources, or even with the causes of economic growth – though he was interested in these problems.

Instead, his main preoccupation was much wider: with the conditions necessary for attaining human freedom. He approached this through a study of history. He believed that there was a pattern of development in history; that one epoch would follow another. Class plays a vital role in these developments. Thus in feudalism power was held by the owners of land who held economic and therefore political power while the serfs owned little or no land and so had little or no power. In feudalism, the serfs produce enough for their own subsistence and have some control over the means of production. However, they are forced politically to produce a surplus above their subsistence requirements. This surplus is then taken from them by the lords who have the legal power to do this.

In the nineteenth century, the power of land was overthrown by the rise of the industrialists, at least in Western Europe and the USA. The power of industry transformed the world. In many ways Marx admired the achievements of the capitalists. In *The Communist Manefesto*, he wrote that 'in scarce one hundred years' they had 'created more massive and more colossal productive forces than have all the proceeding generations together'. But there was a price to pay for this: humanity became enslaved by the impersonal forces of the market. Most people had nothing to sell but their labour. Under capitalism, workers have only their labour power to sell – they do not own the means of production. They produce a surplus that is extracted by the owners of capital; property rights give them the legal power to do this.

Over time, the natural barriers to human development tend to disappear, but are replaced by obstacles imposed by the type of society people live in. Thus Marx argued that people are enslaved under capitalism by their dependence on money and capital. However, this would end as workers became more politically aware (in Marx and Engels's words they had 'nothing to lose but their chains'). As profits fell and crises multiplied, capitalism would be replaced by an epoch of free individuality. Marx wrote very little about this stage of human development; his focus was on the analysis of capitalist society.

In other words, over time society undergoes a series of stages. These are characterised by different forms of property. In feudal society, the serfs were exploited; in contemporary capitalist society the workers own little or no property. They are forced to sell their labour to the owners of capital and are exploited by this class. Each of these developments generates the conditions for the next stage. Thus for Marx 'The history of all hitherto existing society is the history of class struggles'. The economic structure of society explains all other aspects of society. This includes the law, the education system, even the dominant values and beliefs of the society. For example, in capitalist societies, everyone is supposed to be equal before the law, but in reality it helps if you are rich. Moreover, the guiding principle of the law is to protect property rights and to enforce contracts that favour the owners of capital rather than the workers.

Marx and economics

So much for the background. So far as economics was concerned, Marx's starting point was neo-classical economics as it existed when he wrote. Marx read the works of economists such as Smith and Ricardo, but died before Marshall developed recognised concepts such as demand and supply. For Marx, the heart of the matter was profit. The rate of profit is the driving force of capitalist production; nothing will be produced unless the capitalist believes that it will be profitable. So even if society needs cleaner water, more medicines or a cleaner environment, capitalists will not provide them unless there is a profit or they are forced to do so by the law.

A good starting point for Marxian economics is his theory of value since this is the underlying reason why workers are exploited. According to Marx, commodities are exchanged in proportion to the socially necessary labour needed to produce them. In capitalism, labour power is a commodity like any other commodity, that is, it is bought and sold in the market. This labour can be divided up into three parts. The first is the labour needed to make the machines and raw materials used to make the commodity. Marx called this 'constant capital' since it does not rise in the course of production, but only transfers some of its own value to the commodity it is used to produce. For example, in producing a chair, the constant capital is the value of the wood and the machinery used to make the chair. The second component of labour he called 'variable capital' – the labour required to produce the goods needed by the workers and their families. The third component is called 'surplus value' – the amount taken by the capitalist who owns the means of production. This gives them the power to force employees to work longer than is needed to sustain themselves and their families – the basis of the capitalist's profits and the engine of economic growth. Put simply, the owners of the means of production take some of the value of the products made by workers and appropriate it for themselves. They then invest this in more raw materials and machinery, so creating more profit at the expense of workers.

One reason that capitalists are able to do this is the existence of a 'reserve army of labour' which can be brought into and taken out of the labour market as economic circumstances alter. The result of technical change and capital accumulation, which mean that fewer workers are needed to produce a given amount of output, is that there is often a surplus of labour – a reserve army. Moreover, when economies boom and labour is in short supply, it is augmented by immigration and by encouraging women into the labour market. The existence of this reserve army of labour means that there is competition for jobs which in the long run prevents wages rising above the subsistence level. (Note that in Marxian economics, 'subsistence level' does not mean just enough food to exist; rather it means a cultural minimum, plus the expenses of education and training. This will vary over time.) When there is no need for a reserve, women are encouraged to be home-makers and immigration is discouraged.

Marx also developed theories about unemployment. In the first place, this was beneficial for employers since it gave power to owners rather than workers; if there are five applicants for every vacancy, then trade unions will be weak and employers strong. However, at the heart of his theory of unemployment was the notion of crisis. For him, crisis was an inevitable part of the system. For example, competition between capitalists meant that some sectors of the economy would suffer from falling sales and be forced to dismiss workers. Moreover, capitalist production relies on profits and these will tend to fall over time as machinery replaces workers. Also, the nature of the competitive system means that large firms tend to drive small ones out of business; for example, the number of small shopkeepers has greatly diminished as supermarkets have taken over. As time passes, large firms will become more dominant throughout the economy, and crises will result as smaller firms go out of business and even large firms suffer from growing international competition. The result will be unemployment.

Falling profits are the main cause of unemployment in two specific ways. At certain points in the economic cycle, workers will lack the purchasing power to buy all the goods that are produced. This may occur, for example, because firms have paid low wages in order to increase profits. The result is that firms can make goods but cannot sell them because workers do not have the money. Marx called this a 'crisis of realisation' since capitalists cannot realise their profits. Put another way, as the reserve army of labour increases, capitalists find it increasingly difficult to convert their surplus into profit. This is very similar to

Keynes's analysis when he argued that unemployment could be caused by too little aggregate demand.

So, crisis and unemployment can result when workers are paid too little. But the same result will occur when workers are paid too much. When workers are strong, capitalists cannot work their labour force hard enough to generate enough surplus value. In this case there will be a 'crisis of accumulation' since capitalists cannot produce sufficient profit to finance new investment and production. The result: unemployment. In other words, when workers are in a strong position (when the reserve army of labour is small) it takes a longer part of the working day for labour to produce the output of commodities equal to the subsistence wage. This leaves less surplus labour time. In essence, the rate of exploitation falls. So, when wages are too high or too low, the result is unemployment. And since there is no automatic mechanism to make wages just the right level, unemployment is a built-in feature of the system.

So there are really three Marxian approaches to crises. At the first stage, rapid economic growth may push up real wages, cutting profits so that firms cannot invest. This will cause firms to cut their labour force, since workers will not be needed to produce raw materials and investment goods. The result: a rise in unemployment, forcing down wages. Crisis may also occur in the second stage. Technical progress may induce technological unemployment. According to Marx, it will certainly cause cyclical instability as the ratio of machinery to labour changes over time since this will cause profits to rise and fall generating instability and unemployment. Crises may also occur at the third stage. If real wages fall, for example, because of a rise in the size of the reserve army of labour, then workers will not be able to buy the goods and a crisis of underconsumption will occur – a Keynesian-type crisis of inadequate demand.

International factors
So, you may ask, if crises are inevitable, why have living standards risen in countries such as the UK?

In order to answer this, we need to bring in international factors. Cheap raw materials from less developed countries can lower costs in developed countries, so preventing a fall in the rate of profit. In addition, developing countries can provide a market for goods produced in developed countries, so preventing a crisis of underconsumption. Finally, new sources of investment in the Third World can prevent imbalances between sectors of the capitalist core economies. Instead of free trade being to the advantage of everyone, as Ricardo had argued, in the Marxian view trade is really determined by the profit requirements of large capitalist firms who seek new markets, cheap raw materials and investment opportunities. This mitigates but does not eliminate crisis in the advanced industrial economies.

So, the relations between rich and poor countries are important for Marxian economists. Marx wrote very little on what was then called 'imperialism'. It was later writers who developed the notion that crises could be delayed. Although there is disagreement among them, many Marxian economists would argue that the West is rich *because* the Third World is poor. Countries in Africa, Asia and South America are forced by the system to produce raw materials and primary products such as tea and coffee. The reason why this exploitation can take place is that capitalist economies can use their economic and political power – and occasionally their military power – to structure the world economic system to their benefit. In Marxian analysis, this is called dependency theory – in a phrase, 'the development of underdevelopment'. As more and more countries produce these commodities, their price falls. Their living standards fall – or are kept low – whilst ours in the west rise since we benefit from cheap products produced by low-cost labour. In this view, economic backwardness is the product of the capitalist system. Although less developed countries have thrown off colonial rule, they are still politically and economically dependent. This is reinforced by the West's direct ownership of assets in poor countries, by technical domi-nation and by the dependency caused by the debts poor countries owe to the rich. The core of this dependency theory is that a large part of the economic surplus of poor countries is taken by the advanced capitalist countries and so is not available to use for economic development.

In this section we have looked at just a few aspects of Marxian economic analysis. We have concentrated on three aspects: the theory of value and exploitation, crisis and unemployment, and the interna-tional aspect. In many ways this gives an inadequate description of Marxian economics, but it is enough to show that it provides a radical alternative to conventional approaches.

▶ The environmental critique of conventional economics

If Marxian economics is well-developed and wide-ranging, the envi-ronmental critique is relatively new and narrow, but is growing in influence. It has a much less developed theoretical base than the Marxian approach, and fundamentally represents a critique of the values underpinning most economic analysis. For example, Robertson (1998, p. 9) writes:

> A great variety of activities now reflect people's growing commitment to people centred, ecologically sustainable development – new lifestyles, new technologies, new enterprises, new approaches to business management, and so on. On the negative side, the conventional ways of evaluating economic decisions and progress are deeply misconceived, and the present economic system has inherent tendencies to destroy the natural environment, to destroy community, to transfer wealth from poor to rich, to marginalise people, communities and cultures, to erode and deny the sense of the spiritual or sacred and to create learned incapacity and helplessness.

In contrast, the principles of the environmentalist approach include:

- systematic empowerment of people. Conventional economics often assumes that selfishness and competitiveness dominate human nature; the environmental approach emphasises altruism and co-operation
- systematic conservation of resources and environment
- evolution from a 'wealth of nations' model of economic life to a one world model, and from to-day's international economy to a decentralising multi-level one world economic system;
- restoration of political and ethical choice to a central place in economic life and thought, based on respect on qualitative values . . . and
- respect for feminine values, not just masculine ones.(Robertson, 1998, p. 15)

Two diagrams, Figures 4.1 and 4.2, contrast the different approaches. 'Conventional' economics is illustrated in Figure 4.1. As shown, it is a linear system. Raw materials are taken from the earth and treated as free (though, of course, there are costs involved in extraction). These are then processed, sold and consumed. Wastes are created at almost all these stages, and these are then usually dumped, treating the earth as a sink. Moreover many, probably most, of the natural resources that are used are non-renewable. Oil is an example. Once used up it can never be replaced.

In contrast, in the environmentalist approach the earth is treated as the most valuable resource. The economic system is no longer treated as external to the natural world, but as part of it. This is done by creating a circular system, with waste products continually being recycled. People extracting materials from the earth, or using it as a dump, pay

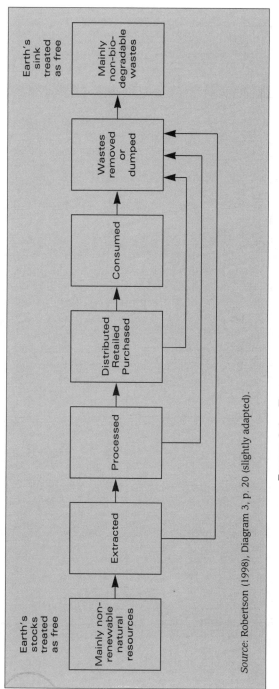

Source: Robertson (1998), Diagram 3, p. 20 (slightly adapted).

FIGURE 4.1 THE ECONOMIC SYSTEM: LINEAR MODE

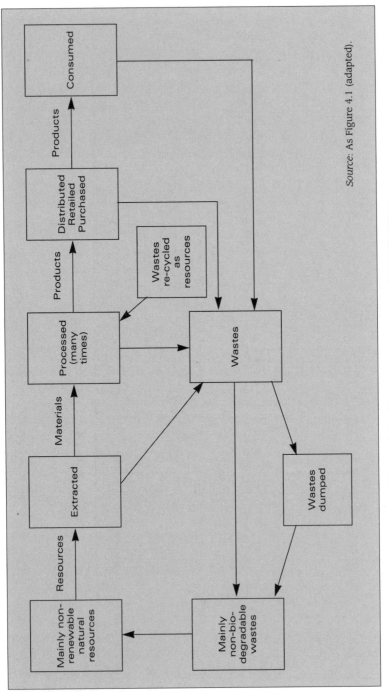

FIGURE 4.2 THE ECONOMIC SYSTEM: CIRCULAR MODE

Source: As Figure 4.1 (adapted).

for the privilege. This creates an incentive to use fewer raw materials and to make better use of those that are extracted. The essential idea is that resource efficiency can be improved by reducing energy and materials wastage at every stage in the production – consumption cycle. Existing and new technologies can achieve this: the result can be more and better goods and services whilst using up fewer resources.

This 'new' economics seeks to replace the present notion of economic progress with one that is not only people-centred but also earth-centred. Traditional economics encourages exploitation of both people and nature. The rich and powerful should pay for their use of resources and enjoyment of monetary values which are created by nature and society. The present system ensures that it is the rich that benefit and the poor who suffer from unsustainable development.

Environmentalist proposals
It is not possible here to examine all the implications of this analysis, but the overall thrust can be exemplified by looking at a few aspects.

The production of food is one example. Efficiency in this context is usually measured by comparing the output with the inputs, mainly labour, used to produce it. For environmentalists, a better measure would be to compare the calorific value of the food produced and the materials used to produce it. Environmentalists claim that the present system of food production damages the environment by its insistence on large-scale production methods, using mass spraying of pesticides. The introduction of genetically modified foods is another threat. The present system also fails to eliminate hunger, even in rich countries, whilst hunger is a common feature of life in poor ones. There are many reasons for this: one is that in many countries, the best land is used to produce export-oriented crops whilst local people have insufficient land to grow their food. Even when they have access to land, the landowners take a large proportion of the crop as rent.

Instead of this system, there should be more emphasis on self-reliant rural communities, for example, by encouraging people to grow their own food even in richer countries. This emphasis on local development is an important feature of environmental economics. It emphasises greater local economic self-reliance which will contribute to social well-being as well as to sustainability and economic efficiency. One benefit of this is that it will reduce the huge number of lorries carrying food from one part of the country to another.

Trade can also be used to exemplify this environmentalist approach. At present, multinational corporations conduct a huge proportion of international trade. These have a vested interest in continuing the present system, as do international institutions such as the World Bank, the World Trade Organisation (WTO) and the International Monetary Fund (IMF). Environmentalists suggest that instead of encouraging free trade we should move to a system which uses a smaller share of the world's natural resources and a more efficient use of human resources. They argue that unregulated free trade harms the environment. For example, the USA tried to restrict the importation of tuna from Mexico since the methods used to catch the fish involved the death of dolphins that were also caught in the fishing nets. The USA also acted to protect the interests of its farmers by using the World Trade Organisation to oppose European Union attempts to restrict the importation of American beef that had been treated with growth hormones. 'Free' trade also restricts the development of poorer countries. In part, this is the 'infant industries' argument discussed earlier (p. 45). One feature of conventional economic development is that it increases the power of some people over others. Firms such as Monsanto which control genetically modified seeds will have power over those who use the seeds. This line of criticism is in line with the Marxian approach; where it differs, according to the environmentalists, is that the Marxian analysis leads to a concentration of state power whilst environmentalists want power to be held locally.

A third example will also illustrate the thrust of this approach. Its supporters argue that the present tax system has many undesirable features. Many taxes fall on employment, incomes and saving. They therefore discourage these desirable activities. For example, both workers and their employers pay National Insurance contributions. This tax therefore inhibits people from working since it makes work less worthwhile, and it increases the cost to firms when they employ workers. Instead, supporters of this approach argue that taxes should encourage desirable activities and fall instead on activities that deplete natural resources, or more generally, on the use of natural resources such as the ability of the earth to absorb waste and pollution. Wherever possible, such taxes should be applied upstream – on producers rather than consumers. The introduction of a tax on gas had one desirable feature – it discouraged the use of this non-renewable resource – but it was flawed in that it was paid by consumers. Moreover, it placed a heavy burden on the poor for whom heating takes up a relatively large part of total spending. Instead of this, environmentalists argue that there should be taxes on nuclear energy and fossil fuels collected at source. This would raise the cost of using energy, so decreasing its use and reducing pollution. Firms could be compensated by cuts in other taxes such as National Insurance. This suggestion is opposed by firms using a large amount of energy, mainly in manufacturing, on the grounds that it would reduce their international competitiveness. Many environmentalists also suggest that revenue from such taxes should be used progressively, that is, be used to benefit the poor. At present, much public spending actually exacerbates problems. For example, we spend more on roads than on rail. Similarly, enormous sums of public money have been spent on research into nuclear energy; if this had been spent on research into energy conservation, it would have had huge benefits in terms of the environment. Another example is the tax advantages given to company cars. These encourage excessive use of private as compared to public transport. Similarly, a firm is not taxed for offering its staff free parking, but would be if it offered free or subsidised public transport.

One example of an environmentally desirable tax, announced in the budget of 1994, is that on dumping waste in landfill sites. This aims to apply the 'polluter pays' principle and to promote a more sustainable approach to waste management. The amount of tax depended on weight so that 'inactive waste' was charged at a rate of £2 a tonne whilst less desirable waste faced a tax of £7 a tonne. In order to compensate firms for this tax, it was accompanied by a reduction in the rate of employers' National Insurance contributions. It therefore represents a step towards the transfer of taxation away from labour and towards pollution and resource use. However, there are limits to the expansion of this tax. If the rates were raised too high, there would be an incentive to fly-tip, that is, to dump rubbish anywhere rather than in approved sites, so creating more pollution.

One of the underlying themes of this approach to economics is the idea of sustainability. Environmentalists are unhappy with the idea of unlimited economic growth, as currently undertaken, as a policy goal. Instead they advocate the idea of 'sustainable development'; that is, development that meets the needs of the present without compromising the ability of future generations to meet their own needs. Put simply, our generation should not be so determined to enjoy economic growth that we use up the world's resources, leaving our descendants with insufficient. Oil is a good example. At present rates of oil use, the world's known reserves of oil will run out in a few decades (though estimates of reserves are never accurate).

Economic indicators

In economic life, if things cannot be counted, they are often ignored. Therefore, in order to make environmental progress, we need to measure environmental aspects of the economy. At present, though there has been some progress, this is largely ignored. The conventional measure of how the economy is doing is gross national product (GNP) or its very similar relation gross domestic product (GDP) (the difference between national and domestic is net income received from ownership of assets from abroad which is included in national but not domestic). This was discussed briefly in Chapter 2 (p. 37). Its advantage is that it gives us a measure of the output of an economy which can then be used in many ways, for example, to compare rates of economic growth with those in the past and to make international comparisons. However, GNP statistics have many limitations. In the first place, the figures are always inaccurate – not surprising given the task of trying to measure the output of every firm and individual in the country. Moreover, they do not include unpaid work so that housework is not included and neither are DIY activities. This means that money spent on producing nuclear weapons or advertising cigarettes is counted, but food and flowers grown in allotments are excluded.

GNP statistics have particular limitations so far as the environment is concerned. Monies spent correcting environmental damage actually add to GNP and make it seem that the country is better off, when the opposite may be the case. For example, people forced to double-glaze their house to reduce noise from increased road traffic will be no better off than they were prior to the traffic increase, but the money spent on double glazing will contribute to a rise in GNP. Hence, the actual measure of GNP overstates the true measure because it ignores the costs of environmental damage. Similarly, if a forest is chopped down, the monetary value of the forest is included in the statistics, but nothing is subtracted to reflect the loss of the forest. This also applies to the extraction of gas, oil and coal. Another environmental limitation of GNP statistics is that the pollution that is generated by industry and not mitigated reduces welfare, but this reduction is not subtracted from the statistics.

At the heart of this line of approach is the idea that money prices do not provide an objective measure of value – as conventional economics assumes; rather they are a socially constructed measure of value reflecting political values and priorities.

So, these limitations in official measures of economic activity have led to efforts to develop alternatives. In this approach, a good indicator should have several qualities. It should be readily available – it is no use suggesting some measure that would be very difficult or expensive to construct. Moreover, the indicator should be about something measurable – such things as happiness, whilst desirable, are not easily measured. It should also be easy to understand and measure something important – it is often easier to measure trivial things than ones that matter. Finally, a good indicator should allow comparisons across time and space. In other words, it should measure key elements of sustainable development and so encourage measurable progress to be made.

The best-known alternative to GNP – best-known to those in the field, but not to others – is an indicator called the human development index (HDI). This is based on national averages of three indicators: longevity, which uses statistics on life expectancy at birth; educational attainment, which is measured by a combination of adult literacy and enrolment ratios at primary, secondary and tertiary levels; and GDP per head. These statistics are then converted into an index form (indexes are explained in Chapter 5 pp. 109–11) to give an average of the three measures. Each country then scores between 0.00 and 1.00, with a higher score suggesting a higher level of human development.

The main advantages of the HDI are that it is simple – just one number – and that it is broader than GNP, but it has several limitations. For example, since it incorporates GNP statistics, the inadequacies of that measure are reproduced. Moreover, in many countries statistics on life expectancy and educational attainment are not very accurate. Again, the HDI says nothing about the environmental aspects of human development.

One difficulty of constructing measures of environmental progress is that statistics are not readily available, not least because many aspects of the environment are difficult to measure. For example, how should we measure the costs of ozone depletion or of noise pollution? Despite the problems, several efforts have been made. For example, Jackson *et al.* (1997) have attempted to measure changes in sustainable economic welfare in the UK in the period 1950–96. A brief summary of their work is given in Table 4.1.

One clear conclusion emerges from this table: GDP per head has risen far more quickly than overall economic welfare. However, before we can accept this estimate, we need to look in a bit more detail at how the authors constructed the table. Their measure of sustainable economic welfare was made up by combining nearly twenty variables, including estimates for long-term environmental damage, ozone

TABLE 4.1 SUSTAINABLE ECONOMIC WELFARE IN THE UK, 1950–96

Year	GDP per head £	Sustainable economic welfare £ per head
1950	3507	1800
1960	4392	2015
1970	5531	2303
1980	6538	2920
1990	8343	2623
1996	8890	2249

Source: Jackson, T., Marks, N., Ralls, J. and Stymne, S. (1997) *Sustainable Economic Welfare in the UK 1950–1996*, Centre for Environmental Strategy, University of Surrey.

depletion costs, costs of car accidents and various types of pollution. They made strenuous efforts to quantify these variables. To give just two examples: their estimate of ozone depletion was arrived at by estimating consumption of CFCs (the chemicals which cause ozone depletion) and giving this a cost of £30 per kilo (the £30 is arrived at by adapting an earlier American study). They estimated noise pollution by using two pieces of research, one that measured increases in noise pollution over time and another that attempted to estimate its cost. Clearly, all these variables are very difficult to measure, and estimates of their costs are subject to a great deal of subjectivity. This estimate must therefore be regarded as a heroic endeavour rather than as a precise calculation. Nevertheless, it indicates very clearly that there is a considerable difference between economic welfare that relies just on GDP statistics and one that incorporates environmental measures.

▶ A feminist critique

Feminist economics is one aspect of the feminist movement that grew rapidly in the 1960s. There were several reasons: women were entering higher education in greater numbers and it was becoming normal for women to remain in the labour market, even after marriage. This was combined with a feeling that contemporary social arrangements were unfair to women. Going out to work had a twofold effect. It gave women greater financial independence, but it also gave them double responsibilities – for bringing up children as well as working.

Feminist economists reflected these concerns. They argued that neo-classical economics often assumed that men were the breadwinners and women's earnings were secondary. Other feminist economists attacked the 'New Home Economics' which argued that it was efficient for women to concentrate on housework since they had greater experience in this area, and this made them more efficient. They also criticised Marxian economics for assuming genderless notions of the proletariat (that is, the workers).

Feminist economists challenge several rarely stated assumptions that underlie neo-classical economics. One is that women are married and dependent. When writing about the labour market, many economists ignored the fact that men and women were often different sorts of worker and assumed that the male pattern of continual full-time employment was the norm to which all workers conformed. Women were assumed to be financially dependent on their husbands and worked for 'pin money'. Their job was to bring up children and look after their husband when he came home from work, but this 'job' was not examined for a long time within the main body of economic thought – women were invisible. This meant that if they did go out to work, their family would suffer and they would be less efficient than men. Hence their lower wages reflected their lower productivity.

Feminist economists pointed out that many women were the chief breadwinners, even when married, and that many unmarried women were responsible for bringing up children. Moreover, the idea of a family wage earned by men was a protection of male privilege and also gave men power in the home, since money means power. These challenges have had considerable effect. Most modern economists would not make such crass assumptions, though these views still underlie a good deal of economics.

The feminist critique has had influence on policy. For example, the Equal Pay Acts that attempted to end the practice of paying women less than men owe much to the arguments of feminists. Similarly, the introduction of a national minimum wage in the UK chiefly benefited women, since the majority of low earners are women.

One thrust of this feminist approach has been to examine economics textbooks. Though the position is changing, most economists are men, and certainly the overwhelming majority of senior economists are men. Consequently it is not surprising that feminist concerns have often been marginalised. For many years, the concerns just discussed dominated introductory economics. For example, when discussing workers, the authors used words such as 'he' or 'him' rather than using less discriminatory words such as 'they', or adopting the approach which we have often used, of using 'she' to illustrate points. More recent texts have tended to use this inclusive language and to provide examples of both men and women in their case studies.

Despite this progress, there are still many inadequacies in introductory textbooks, and you should look out for these when reading. For example, when topics such as poverty are discussed, do the examples include women (and ethnic minorities)? Does the text explicitly discuss the role of women in the productive process?

Household production and specialisation

There is overwhelming evidence that when a couple live together, it is the women who do most of the household tasks. Why is this?

One answer, now largely discredited, is that women are biologically more suited to these tasks. Even a simplistic analysis would find it hard to produce evidence that a woman's body makes her superior in washing or ironing. A more sophisticated argument has already been touched upon: the advantages of the division of labour. In the economy as a whole, there is no doubt that this leads to greater efficiency. Specialised workers are usually much more efficient than those who try to do many jobs. If you had to have brain surgery, would you prefer to have it done by a brain surgeon or by a GP? This line of argument has led some economists to suggest that it is efficient for women to specialise in household tasks while men specialise in money-making in the paid labour market. On average, men earn more than women, so the opportunity cost for a man devoting time to household chores is greater than if a women used her time to do them. In this way, the principle of comparative advantage can be used to justify the stereotype of the 'ideal' family – man the breadwinner, woman the homemaker.

Feminist economists make several criticisms of this approach. In the first place, only a minority of households follow this pattern of husband and wife, with the man being the earner. So, even if the analysis had some truth, it would only apply to a minority of households. Then, there are many disadvantages associated with the division of labour, particularly within a family. In the first place the partner who concentrates on the home activities may not be learning any marketable skills, whilst the one engaged in the paid labour market can expect to acquire skills and promotion. Now in the UK there is about one divorce for every two marriages. This means that when divorce occurs, the partner who has concentrated on domestic tasks is at a considerable disadvantage when entering the world of paid work (though some feminist economists argue that skills such as time management, negotiation and multi-tasking are learned in a domestic context and are valuable in the labour market.) Another disadvantage of the division of labour which is true of almost all work, paid or not, is that doing a specialised task can be very boring. This is true of almost all assembly-line work, for example, and it is true of much household work. It is therefore inequitable for one partner to have to specialise in boring work whilst the other can experience the variety which often comes with paid work. Feminist economists are also concerned with the decision-making process within households. Traditional economic theory assumes that rational men and women – 'economic actors', make choices that will maximise their utility, – that is their economic welfare. However, in practice women's choice is heavily constrained by social pressures. Women are expected to do most of the household tasks, and in particular to take most of the responsibility for bringing up children. Even if both parents go out to work, if a child falls ill, it is usually the woman who is expected to look after the child. Given these social pressures, it is very difficult for a woman's choice to be undertaken freely. Her choice may reflect society pressure and social custom rather than her welfare maximisation.

Feminists argue that household work, mainly done by women, is largely ignored in 'official' economics, that is, that presented in official statistics such as measurement of national output. Instead, the economy which is presented is that which is visible, male-dominated and paid for in cash, rather than the full range of human economic endeavour. In official statistics, a meal bought in a shop counts as part of national output; one cooked at home does not. Similarly, time spent cleaning offices is part of the market economy whilst time spent cleaning at home is ignored. Most important of all, time spent bringing up children is not counted. All these activities are largely done by women; consequently, the official statistics ignore huge areas of national output that are done by women. One reason for this is that there is no agreement on how to value such work. It would be possible to estimate the number of hours spent on such activities, though this could never be accurate. But how should time be valued? One answer would be to take a typical wage – £x an hour for cleaning, £y an hour for childcare and so on. Some feminists, whilst welcoming such approaches, fear that it would undervalue women's work because such work is typically low-paid. Moreover, there are concerns about aggregating the unpaid and paid economies. The central interest of feminists is the interaction between the two. The unpaid economy is not just an addition to the market economy; it is central to it.

One useful approach adopted by feminist economists is to develop a three-sector model of the economic world as shown in Figure 4.3. Most economics concentrates on the relationship between markets and states, for example, by building up models of consumer choice, analysing how markets work and arguing about what should be the role of the state in the economy. The reason has been hinted at above: since most economists are men, their models have focused attention on the public sphere where they spend the majority of their working lives as opposed to the household which is paramount for many women. Indeed, for many years, the foundation of economic analysis was the notion of 'economic *man*', a rational, self-interested individual whose decisions were taken to maximise his 'utility' (that is, satisfaction). Economic *man* has largely disappeared, but the central notion is usually still that of self-centred individuals maximising their own welfare.

The three-sector approach suggests that this is inadequate. Men and women differ in their self-interested choices because of their differing relationships to others. In particular, women's role often involves caring for others who are dependent on them. In turn, this constrains women's ability to maximise their own welfare.

The three-sector model is also useful in that it focuses attention on the value of unpaid economic activities that are often undertaken in the household. If the emphasis is on market and price, then unpaid labour is ignored. Many economic models assume that people have to choose between paid work and leisure. But this is not the whole story since it ignores domestic work. This is not only unpaid, it is crucial to the economy. It provides vital inputs into the economy. For example, it is at home that children learn essential skills, such as communication that will be vital in their future life. Similarly, economic life depends on

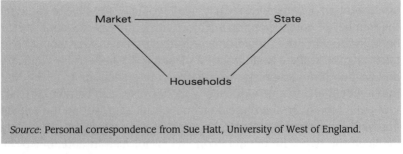

Source: Personal correspondence from Sue Hatt, University of West of England.

FIGURE 4.3   A THREE-SECTOR MODEL OF THE ECONOMY

a shared ethical basis; the foundation of this is also laid at home. This third sector – households – differs from the other two in another way. Whilst the market depends on profits as its motivating force, and the public sector passes laws and makes regulations, the household sector focuses on provisioning. This does not just mean the provision of food; it also includes the provision of love and care. This means that the motivating force is not self-interest, but altruism, a concept that does not always fit easily into mainstream neo-classical economics.

Women in the labour market
For most of the twentieth century, only about a third of women in the UK were active participants in the labour market and this low participation rate was true of many other European countries. These were mainly unmarried women – indeed, in some occupations, women were forced to resign if they got married. Women's participation increased during the Second World War and increased significantly in the last two or three decades of the twentieth century, particularly in the UK and in Scandinavian countries. For example, in the UK between 1988 and 1998, the economic activity rate for women of working age increased from 70 per cent to 72 per cent whilst for men it fell from 88 per cent to 84 per cent. One reason for this fall is that high unemployment caused some men to leave the labour force, recognising that they would never work again.

The biggest change was the trend for women with young children to be economically active since in the same period the economic activity rate for women with children under five rose from 45 per cent to 55 per cent (Thair and Risdon, 1999, p. 103). ('Economically active' is the sum of those in employment plus the unemployed.)

We can explain these trends in a typical way for economists – by analysing demand and supply factors. Demand for women workers has risen for several reasons. Increasing prosperity means an increase in the demand for labour in general and women have benefited from this. Moreover, a large part of the rise in demand has been in services where women form a large part of the workforce. For example, there have been large rises in industries such as education and health. Another reason is that there has been a huge rise in part-time jobs, and women are more likely to take this kind of job. Finally, more women now have higher levels of education, and high levels of education are strongly linked to increased levels of labour force participation.

Supply-side factors also explain the rise in women's labour force participation. One is that real wages have increased, and just as we would expect a rise in the price of a good to lead to an increase in supply (remember, supply curves rise up to the right), so we would expect higher wages to lead to a rise in supply. This supply-side effect has been reinforced by demographic changes such as the rise in the divorce rate, which means that more women have to earn their own living. Technology has also had an effect. Domestic appliances such as washing machines and the availability of ready-cooked meals mean that less time needs to be spent on domestic tasks. And finally, these changes have changed attitudes to women workers. It is now socially acceptable, indeed expected, for married women to go out to work.

Women at work
Look at these two lists of jobs. Can you spot the differences?

Secretary	Company director
Nurse	Surgeon
Care assistant	Mechanic
Checkout assistant	Pilot
Receptionist	Train driver
Nursery teacher	Head teacher

I hope that you found it easy; the jobs in the left-hand side column are overwhelmingly done by women, those on the right by men. And, of course, those on the left tend to be less well paid than those on the right.

There are several theories that try to explain this. One suggests that women are somehow naturally more suited for some jobs. This is not very plausible; for example, when typewriters were first invented, secretaries were overwhelmingly men. This could not have happened if men were not suited for the job. A better explanation is that there are very strong social pressures on women, and to a lesser extent on men, to enter certain careers. If you ask girls as young as five what they want to be when they grow up, a large proportion will reply that they want to be nurses. This suggests that expectations are formed early in life and have a significant effect on later career choice.

This occupational differentiation is one reason why women, on average, earn less than men. This is illustrated in Figure 4.4. There are several points to note about this figure. One is that the earnings of both men and women have risen over the years. One reason for this is inflation; this causes wages to rise as well as prices. Another reason is that real incomes have risen; even after taking inflation into account people now earn more than they did in the 1980s.

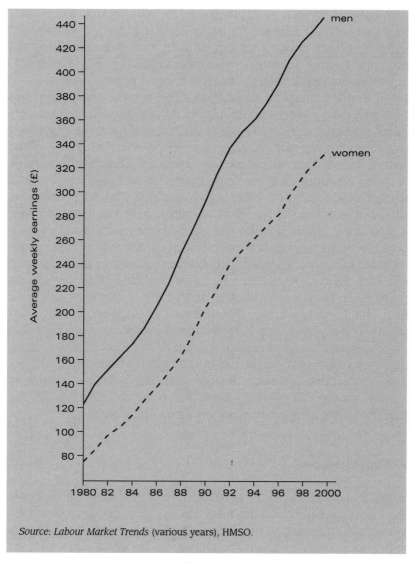

Source: *Labour Market Trends* (various years), HMSO.

FIGURE 4.4 WEEKLY EARNINGS OF MEN AND WOMEN

From our point of view, however, the crucial factor is that men's wages are constantly higher than women's, though the relative difference is narrowing. At the beginning of the 1980s women's wages were about 64 per cent of men's; at the end of the 1990s this had risen to about 72 per cent.

So, why do women earn less than men? One reason has already been mentioned – women tend to take jobs in certain occupations, and these tend to be poorly paid jobs. In turn, one reason why they are poorly paid is that women's choice means that there is a large supply of workers for particular jobs, and this brings down the wage. This is not a complete explanation since women tend to earn less than men even in the same occupation. For example, women teachers on average tend to earn less than men. There are many explanations of women's lower pay; here we can only summarise a few of the factors. One is that, as we saw in Chapter 1, there is a close link between education and earnings. Until very recently, women have tended to achieve lower educational standards than men. Hence we should expect them to have lower earnings. In recent years however, women have achieved equal and often higher educational qualifications, so we should expect a narrowing of differentials in future years.

Other factors remain which may keep women's earnings at a lower rate than men's. They often have career breaks and so lose out on promotions. They are also likely to receive less on-the-job training. If a man is offered promotion that requires a geographical move, his partner is likely to give up her job and follow him, so requiring her to make a fresh start. And despite legislation outlawing discrimination, there is no doubt that it continues to work against women in the labour market. All these are social factors, reflecting women's position in society, and are difficult to change. Hence, we can expect only slow removal of wage differentials between men and women.

▶ Conclusion

In this chapter we have tried to outline three contrasting approaches to the 'conventional' economics taught in most universities. Our reason is twofold. In recent years, there has been growing dissatisfaction within the economics profession with some aspects of economics; for example, that it is too narrow, too concerned with measurement and quantification. Our three critiques offer alternative perspectives and reflect the fact that many economics courses do now emphasise feminist and environmental concerns (though Marxian economics is often offered just as an option).

The second reason for including this chapter is to encourage you to think about what you read. When you read an economics book (including this – perhaps especially this), you should always assess what you read, for example, by asking to yourself, 'What is the evidence? What does this assume?'

Let us end by giving you three questions to answer – there are no right answers to these; your thoughts are what matter:

1. The Marxian approach is over a hundred years old. If it is so good, why have more economists not adopted it?
2. Is the environmental approach too wishy-washy – full of genuine concerns, but with little real hard data?
3. The feminist approach offers some severe criticisms of traditional economics, but what positive alternatives does it offer?

Alternatively, you could ask of each of these critiques, 'How is it better than the conventional approach?'

References

Jackson,T., Marks, N., Ralls, J. and Stymne, S. (1997) *Sustainable Economic Welfare in the UK*, Centre for Environmental Strategy, University of Surrey.

Robertson, J. (1998) *Transforming Economic Life*, Dartington, Green Books.

Thair, T. and Risdon, A. (1999) 'Women in the labour market', *Labour Market Trends* (March), London, HMSO, pp. 103–27.

Further reading

Ferber, M. A. and Nelson, J. A. (eds) (1993) *Beyond Economic Man, Feminist Theory and Economics*, University of Chicago Press.

Kuiper, E. and Sap, J. (eds) (1995) *Out of the Margin, Feminist Perspectives on Economics*, London, Routledge.

Milward, B. (2000) *Marxian Political Economy*, Basingstoke, Palgrave.

5 Mathematics and Statistics in Economics

It may be a long time since you studied mathematics and you may feel you have forgotten most of it. Or you may be a keen student of mathematics and statistics, waiting with excitement to see their power applied to economics. We have to tell you that the majority of students of economics are not in the latter category. So the key question is 'how much maths do I need to study economics?' Indeed, do you need any mathematical knowledge or ability at all?

The answer is not a simple one, and once again we see economists disagreeing! Many of you will be studying economics for a short time alongside other subjects, seeking a complementarity of ideas from them. Others will wish to pursue mathematical economics courses for some time, eventually being employed in that area. The entry requirements for different economics courses reflect this range, from needing no prior knowledge of mathematics to needing good A level mathematics grades for some degree programmes. So much depends on what areas of economics interest you and how far you wish to take your studies. It is certainly possible to understand many aspects of economic theory and applied economics with very little mathematics.

The first aim of this chapter is to explain how mathematics and statistics are used in economics, and the second is to give you a glimpse of how that occurs in different scenarios. Most importantly, we will try to encourage a willingness to develop your abilities and to have a positive attitude to all the skills that help you understand the subject, including the mathematical ones.

So to look at the first area, how are mathematics and statistics used in economics and what is their value? These are huge questions and ones to which we can only attempt limited answers at this stage, but let us begin.

Economics addresses real problems and to analyse and understand them we often build models of these problems. Usually these models simplify the complexities of the real problem to give us a framework.

For example, we saw one example in Chapter 2 where the demand for a product was affected by its price, the level of people's incomes, advertising and the price and quality of other goods. We simplified this by looking closely at one of these, the price of the product, and later drew a demand curve. The business producing that product would find it an advantage if it knew how the market demand was influenced by these factors and maybe other things as well. How do economists know and understand the market? They build models to do this and communicate their ideas in different ways. So let us consider the 'language' that economists use in discussing models.

We explain our ideas in words, often alongside graphs or diagrams and also using a set of mathematical equations. These three often provide alternative explanations, not competing ones. However, it is the ability to switch from one method of explanation to another that gives clarity to the model. Each method has strengths, the mathematical one giving clarity, and precision, reducing ambiguity and often providing an operational route forward.

However, there is more to maths in economics than providing an alternative explanation or formulation of an economic model. Mathematical and statistical techniques have been used to open up new areas of economic theory, for example in general equilibrium and welfare analysis. It is unlikely, though, that you would meet these areas early in your studies, and for most of you the important issue is the use of maths as an alternative explanation. We will see examples of this later in the chapter.

Statistics provides some powerful tools, contributing to theoretical developments in the empirical testing of theories, and providing a strong way forward in applied economics. As it is difficult to undertake laboratory experiments to test our theories we make great use of real data to do this. For example, we can attempt to check how far consumption expenditure is linked to income after tax in macroeconomics by using national data. Much of these economic data are collected by the government. They are checked, edited and published and made available to the public, they are readily available to students in libraries and some of them are on the Internet.

In Chapter 2 we saw that economists look at the accounts of the country as a whole – the national income accounts. These accounts are a detailed collection of data and the study of economic statistics examines the principles behind the collection, the definitions used and so on, enabling students and researchers to use and interpret the accounts, judging the economic performance of the country. In fact the government and its agencies publish masses of data relating to the economy – for example, data on international trade and transactions in the balance of payments accounts and details of the financial sector in publications from the Bank of England. The ability to dig around in tables, identifying the key features, often does not involve very sophisticated statistical techniques, but can yield much evidence. Knowing about the ways in which data can be presented helps you to read from others' data in their work and also helps you in your work. It is often a simple basic approach that is needed to prevent the statistics from being misinterpreted and then misleading. Economists therefore need to be able to examine data critically to see what they really show.

Mathematical economics is often done as a separate course and aims to teach the application of mathematical principles and logic to economic theory. The aim is not to train mathematicians; nevertheless, the notation and methodology of maths is used, developing general theory rather than precise relationships, numerically defined. For example, optimisation issues in microeconomics can adopt this method. Advocates of mathematical economics claim it gives rigour, elegance and generality to economic theory. How much pre-knowledge of maths do you need to do this? Students of A level mathematics or its equivalent have an advantage, but most economics courses encourage students without that level to do the course and they are then taught the appropriate techniques as and when needed.

That said, you should not proceed to think that mathematics moves economics from the social sciences to a precise exact science. For many of us, it is that uncertainty stemming from the vagaries of human activity that makes it a fascinating subject. If you are approaching economics from an engineering or scientific background, then a mathematical approach will enable you to learn very quickly about the methods of economic reasoning, and discover new applications of mathematical techniques which are useful and fun. We must also add that as some economic models become more complex and refined then more and more mathematics is needed to handle them.

Recently some texts have attempted to integrate the teaching of mathematics and economics, showing applications of techniques, and are problem-driven rather than technique-driven. Previously these sort of texts have not been at beginners' level. We think it is useful to mention the learning methods needed in this area. Wide reading from various texts and articles, often 'skimmed' to give a breadth of ideas and views that you can synthesise and juxtapose, may be appropriate in some aspects of economics, but not in mathematical economics. It is not advised to dip into texts. Rather a careful detailed read of a few pages, probably repeated with examples to follow, is the best learning method. The gradual building up of material is essential and the value of teaching support in this can be high. Sometimes small steps can be stumbling blocks in understanding and it is here that workshops, tutorials, and seminars with access to teachers can be important in giving you a route forward. It can be difficult for students to teach themselves in this area, although there are learning aids available, some of which are now computer-based.

Econometrics is another area of study relevant to this chapter. When economic models have been built and specified, an essential task of the methodology is to test these models against reality. For example, we have mentioned before that there is a theory that consumption expenditure in aggregate is determined by total disposable income in a country. How true is this? At this point we must refer to the actual data for consumption expenditure and disposable income and many skills are needed to do this. Econometrics uses mathematics and statistical inference to evaluate an economic model in this way, and to look at it empirically. A whole set of techniques has been developed for this and the study of econometrics itself can form a substantial part of an economics degree. The answers given by econometricians in their work are seldom absolute, usually expressing the chances of the results being achieved; for example, they may say there is a 99 per cent chance of a particular value occurring. They also express a range of error for their answer and give the probability or chance of that error occurring. Even so the answer may be incorrect; we are dealing with statistical probability.

So at some point in your studies you may have the opportunity to study econometrics, but by that stage it is likely you will have studied some mathematics and statistics as a foundation for it. Much of your work will be aided by the use of computer packages in this. However, it is still economic problems that are the focus of attention for all your econometric techniques.

Students of economics are often advised or required to study statistics. Sometimes the basics are taught early on and the techniques linked up to economic theory at later stages, particularly in econometrics. Often three aspects of statistics are taught: theory, sources and applications. Methods of describing data, probability and inference theory, regression and correlation are typical theories covered. You may also become an expert on the sources of economic data, for example, what data are available and from which organisations, how their data have been collected and defined, and therefore how they may be interpreted. This is always useful in thinking about the wider picture. For example, what has been excluded from the data you examine, either outside the time-frame presented, or maybe the geographical frame? In the third aspect, applications, we are not referring to the use of statistics in econometrics, but the use of descriptive statistics which occurs from week one in your economic studies.

▶ Microeconomics

First of all we will look at how mathematics can help us in our microeconomic analysis of markets that we considered in Chapter 2. The operation of market forces is a key element in microeconomics and much of the analysis is explained by using demand and supply. Whilst it is recognised that the demand for a product is influenced by many things – for example, its price, advertising, the price of competitive products and so on – it is common to begin the analysis by assuming that the single most important factor is the price of the product. We look at the relationship between the quantity demanded of the product and its price in a particular time period. This means we have two variables and we can apply some basic mathematical techniques. Now the relationship between quantity demanded and price may not be linear, that is, the combinations of price and quantity showing demand may not lie on a straight line, but we will simplify our example so that they do.

Let us begin by thinking about a graph with its two axes x and y as shown in Figure 5.1, with the usual convention of x on the horizontal axis and y on the vertical axis. We can imagine a straight line moving around, and taking for example any of the positions in Figure 5.1 as shown. Let us assume the scales on the two axes on the graph are the same.

The first step in pinning down a line is to fix its gradient, at say 0.5. This means the line goes up vertically by half the distance it goes along. It is now able to move only in parallel with itself as shown in Figure 5.2.

The second and final step in identifying a single line and stopping its movement totally is to nail it down on either the x axis or the y axis and it is usually the latter that is chosen, for example, at $y = 3$ on the vertical axis as in Figure 5.3. This is known as its vertical intercept value.

We now have two numerical values: a gradient of 0.5 and a vertical intercept of 3 and we have defined a particular line on the graph. These values are used in the general equation for the straight line $y = mx + c$,

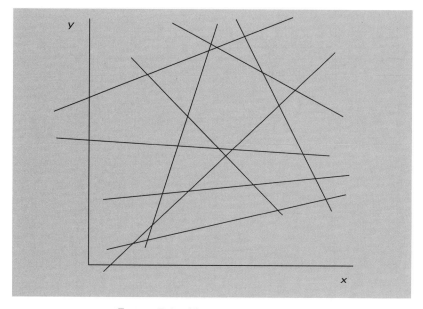

FIGURE 5.1   VARIOUS LINE POSITIONS

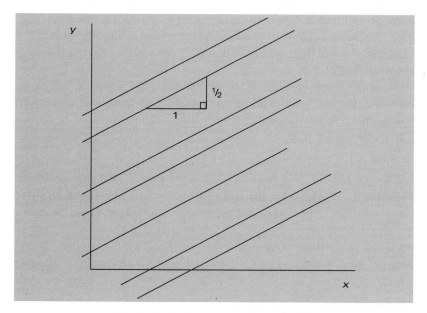

FIGURE 5.2   LINES WITH GRADIENT 0.5

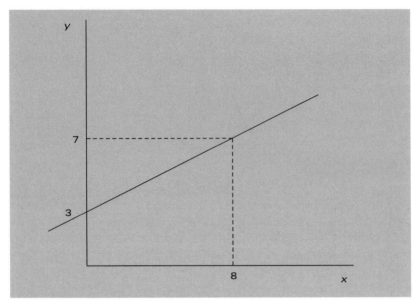

FIGURE 5.3 THE UNIQUE LINE $Y = 0.5 X + 3$

where m and c are our two constants or values for the gradient and the vertical intercept respectively. The x and y are the two variables on the axes. So our line is now defined as $y = 0.5x + 3$, stating that the y variable is always equal to half of the value of the x variable plus 3; for example, if $x = 8$, then we know that $y = 7$; this point lies on the line as shown in Figure 5.3.

We apply these ideas now to our example in Chapter 2 where we have the price of T-shirts and the corresponding quantities demanded and supplied at the different prices.

In Table 2.1 we had:

Price (£)	Quantity demand (q_d) (thousands per month)	Quantity suppled (q_s) (thousands per month)
3	10	2
5	8	4
7	6	6
9	4	8

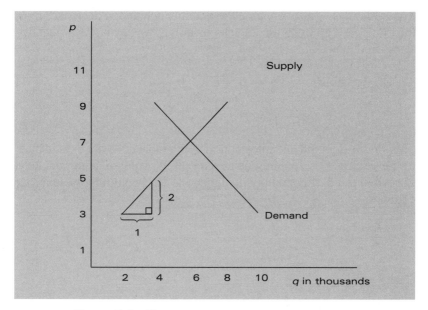

FIGURE 5.4 THE INTERSECTION OF DEMAND AND SUPPLY

Figure 2.1 plotted these points joining them up to give two lines known as the demand and supply curves, (albeit they were straight lines) now shown in Figure 5.4. Relating this to our $y = mx + c$ general equation, what have we got? On the vertical axis we have price, this is our y variable; and on the horizontal axis we have quantity, our x variable. We need to know the values of the gradient m, and the vertical intercept c for each of the two lines, that is, $p = mq_d + c$ for the demand line and $p = mq_s + c$ for the supply line.

On the supply line, the gradient is +1 as every time the price goes up 2, the quantity supplied increases by 2.

So we know $p = q_s + c$, since $m = 1$

The supply line does not extend back to the vertical axis to give us the value of c, so we may find c's value another way. When the price is 3, the quantity supplied is 2, and when the price is 5, the quantity supplied is 4. The difference between price and quantity in both cases is +1, so we can see that c must equal +1.

Our supply curve is $p = q_s + 1$

The derivation of the equation for the demand curve is similar. For this gradient is −1 as every time the quantity demanded decreases by 2, the price goes up by 2; the line slopes down, we say it has a negative slope, and $m = -1$.

So we know $$p = -q_d + c$$

or $$p = c - q_d$$

Again the demand line information in the table does not extend back to the vertical axis enabling us to read off the value of c immediately. But when $p = 3$, the quantity demanded is 10. So putting these in our equation:

$$p = c - q_d$$

$$3 = c - 10$$

makes $c = 13$.

We can check these against another point on the line, say when $p = 5$, and $q_d = 8$,

$$5 = 13 - 8 \text{ (checked correct)}$$

Our demand curve is $p = 13 - q_d$

We can observe in Figure 5.4 where these two lines intersect, but we may use our equations to find the equilibrium price and quantity, where the market forces are balanced.

The equilibrium price will be where the quantities demanded and supplied are equal, that is,

where $q_d = q_s$

So to find the equilibrium price from the equations

Supply curve is $p = q_s + 1$

Demand curve is $p = 13 - q_d$

We simply put $q_d = q_s$

By rearranging the order in the supply equation we know $q_s = p - 1$ and by rearranging the order in the demand equation we know $q_d = 13 - p$ so we can easily put $q_d = q_s$:

$$p - 1 = 13 - p$$

and we have

$$2p = 14$$

$p = 7$, which is the equilibrium price

Either of our two equations will give us the equilibrium quantity at that price, for example, if we put $p = 7$ into our supply line, $p = q_s + 1$, we get $7 = q_s + 1$ and therefore $q_s = 6$ at equilibrium.

We have found the results from the equations we observed in the table and in Figure 5.4. You may say that this is a long way round, and the mathematics does not appear to make the procedures any simpler; in fact it looks more tricky. However, let us go one more step and see if we can show another application and then consider more general issues on this.

Suppose the government imposes minimum wage legislation resulting in wages going up in the manufacture of T-shirts. The suppliers must increase their prices to cover the rise in costs or cut their profits. We will assume that firms are producing efficiently already and cannot reduce the numbers employed. If they attempt to increase their prices by say £1 a T-shirt, does the equilibrium price go up from £7 to £8 or to something different?

From the suppliers' side we see the new desired price as £1 more than the old one, as in Figure 5.5, so we now want the equation of the new supply curve, where we will use q_{s2} as the quantity variable. The gradient remains the same: as price goes up by 2, the quantity still increases by 2, so we have

$$p = q_{s2} + c, \text{ where } m \text{ still equals } +1$$

and when $p = 4$, $q_{s2} = 2$, so $c = 2$, and the new equation after the increase in costs is

$$p = q_{s2} + 2$$

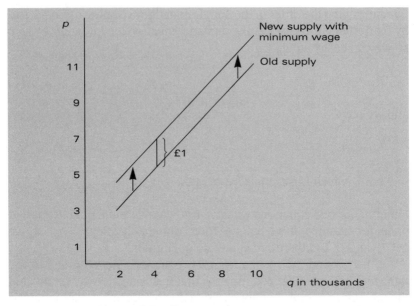

FIGURE 5.5 THE EFFECT OF A HIGHER WAGE

If we put this with the old demand curve, which has not moved, we can find the new equilibrium price in the same way as before.

Supply curve is $p = q_{s2} + 2$ OR $q_{s2} = p - 2$

Demand curve is $p = 13 - q_d$ OR $q_d = 13 - p$

When the market is in equilibrium and the new price is settled, the quantities demanded and supplied are equal, $q_{s2} = q_d$.so

$$p - 2 = 13 - p$$

$$2p = 15$$

$$p = 7.5$$

If we put $p = 7.5$ into our supply equation, the equilibrium quantity brought and sold is now

$$q_{s2} = p - 2$$

$q_{s2} = 7.5 - 2$

$q_{s2} = 5.5$

So the market price has gone up from £7 to £7.50 and the quantity bought and sold has fallen from 6 thousand to 5.5 thousand. Minimum wage legislation had an impact on both price and sales in this case, and our knowledge of the equations and our assumption about the producers' reactions to increases in costs enabled us to give a precise explanation of this impact.

We shall now move to the more general issue on this. We have worked with simple numbers, easily seen on a graph or table, but the convenience and accuracy of this are obvious when the numbers are more daunting and this is usually the reality. The simple techniques we have seen can be applied to many different issues relating to the market analysis of supply and demand, for example, the analysis of shifts of the curves caused by other changes such as the imposition of various taxes or subsidies on goods and services by government, and the effects of tariffs and other matters in international trade and markets. Much of the hard work of these techniques is removed by using the computer, but you still need to grasp what the process is and the meaning of its outcomes. If the relationships are non-linear we have other techniques we may apply, but we are not pursuing them here, and leave them for your later studies. The applications are not confined to microeconomics. The techniques give us precise, fast answers and aid our analysis and understanding of the effects of various changes. But what we have covered should not make you think this route is straightforward; many problems arise along the way.

▶ Macroeconomics

Here we move on from microeconomics to macroeconomics to see more applications. Households spend money on goods and services and government statisticians attempt to measure the total spent by all households and publish their results. Data are also available for the total disposable income received by all households.

Let us consider some simple examples to begin this section.

A country has data for households' expenditure for a run of ten years, and for the same years it has data for disposable income and the rate of interest. We may ask the questions: 'Is there a relationship between the data for the households' consumption expenditure and the disposable income for those years?' and 'Is there a relationship between the data for the households' consumption expenditure and the rate of interest for those years?'

Let us examine Figures 5.6 and 5.7.

What does Figure 5.6 show about the relationship between disposable income and consumption expenditure? There appears to be a pattern – a cluster in an area that seems to follow a line. It looks as though when disposable income is high, consumption expenditure is relatively high and vice versa. What does Figure 5.7 show about the relationship between the rate of interest and consumption expenditure? There seems to be no pattern – the points lie all over the graph and it is difficult to say whether high or low interest rates are associated with high or low levels of consumption expenditure.

If we were given data in one particular year – say the country had disposable income equal to £40 billion, and the rate of interest was 3 per cent – can we estimate consumption expenditure? Which graph would we use and how? The rate of interest in Figure 5.7 gives us a wide range of possibilities at a rate of interest of 3 per cent, from £15b to £45b for consumption expenditure. Such a wide range is not very useful. If we look at Figure 5.6, a value for disposable income of £40b

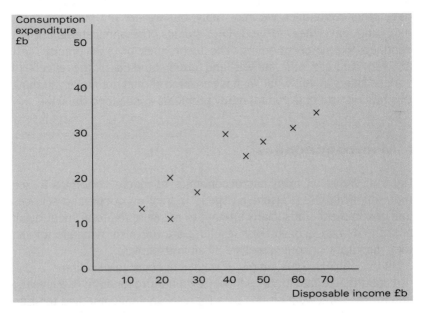

FIGURE 5.6 DATA FOR CONSUMPTION EXPENDITURE AND DISPOSABLE INCOME

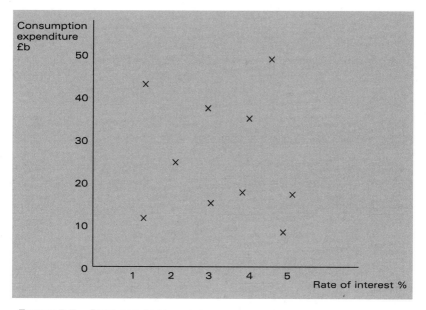

FIGURE 5.7 DATA FOR CONSUMPTION EXPENDITURE AND THE RATE OF INTEREST

gives us consumption expenditure of about £25b–£28b, which is a bit more precise and is therefore more useful.

We can answer these questions simply as we have done, but many techniques have been developed to refine what we have described here and their approach is powerful. What follows is an attempt to introduce you to these methods in a little more detail.

As economists we are interested in the relationship between disposable income (Y_d) and total spending (C). It is possible to take the numbers for these two items in a particular year and show them as a single point on a graph. If we repeat this for a run of say ten years, we end up with a scatter of 10 points as in Figure 5.8, each point referring to a particular year. So what does this scatter diagram show? That in years when disposable income is relatively high, spending by all households referred to as consumption is high and vice versa. Disposable income and consumption expenditure are the variables. We refer to this as a positive relationship between these two variables – they seem to change in the same positive or negative direction.

A word of warning at this stage. This does not show how these two variables are linked, or indeed that they are connected at all. Let us explain. There is a theory in macroeconomics which says that the main determinant of total consumption expenditure is how much money

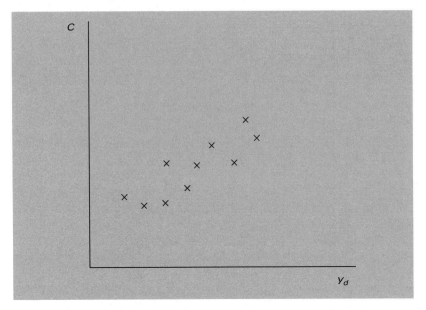

FIGURE 5.8 A SCATTER DIAGRAM SHOWING A POSITIVE RELATIONSHIP

people have in their pockets to spend, that is, disposable income. Advocates of this theory would look at published data for evidence to support this view. But it is possible that consumers' expenditure varies for other reasons and that the positive relationship observed between these two is merely coincidence (although economic theory says otherwise). Already we see how limited this kind of approach may be.

However, let us take it a little further. Is it possible to be more precise mathematically in looking at this scatter diagram? One mathematical technique that may be applied is to calculate a line that is in some way a good fit for the scatter, known as a line of best fit, which goes through the 'middle' of the data. We are saying it is the 'middle' if we look at the vertical distances as in Figure 5.9.

We are using regression techniques. It makes sense in behavioural terms to think of consumption expenditure, C, being dependent on disposable income (Y_d), that is, C is the dependent variable being determined by Y_d the independent variable. It is customary to show the dependent variable on the vertical axis of the graph and the independent variable on the horizontal axis. So it is the best fit for consumption that we search for, as shown in Figure 5.9.

So how can we find this line? It is possible to guess it, as has been done in the graph, simply drawing it in by eye. Obviously this gives a

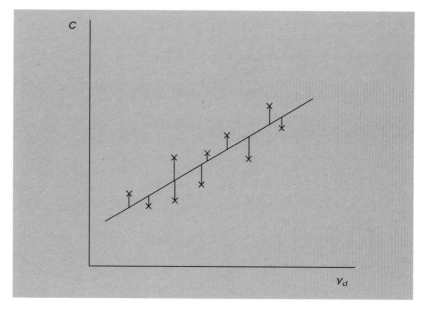

FIGURE 5.9   LINE OF BEST FIT $C = 30 + 0.9\ Y_d$

rough idea, but mathematical techniques can give us a precise answer. If the relationship between C and Y_d is important and is going to be used by practising economists, we need a precise answer.

Returning to our straight line. Consumption (C) is the y variable and disposable income (Y_d) is the x variable.

There are regression techniques that enable us to find the values of m and c for a line of best fit. They are rigorously defined, but we leave that for your later studies. Let us assume we have used them and found the following:

$$C = 30 + 0.9\ Y_d$$

Or in a graph, this is the line that is the best fit, as shown in Figure 5.10. Assume the axes have the same scales.

From Figure 5.10, when $Y_d = 0$, $C = £30$ million. What does this mean? How can households spend when they have no disposable income? Well, there are different reasons for this, but one simple one is that they spend savings they have made previously. What alternative is there – starvation? Of course, these extremes are not practically envisaged, but serve to illustrate the point. The value of 0.9 for the gradient is more enlightening about consumer behaviour: it indicates that if

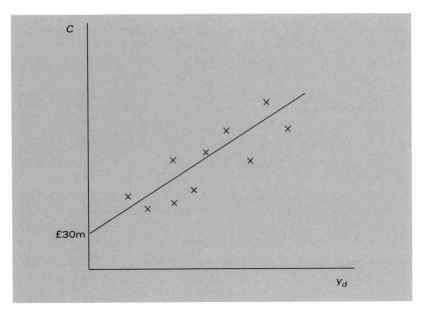

FIGURE 5.10 LINE OF LEAST FIT WITH NUMBERED ORIGIN EQUALS THE GRADIENT

households have an extra amount of disposable income, say £1m in total, they will spend 0.9 of it or 90 per cent of it. So C goes up by £900 000. What happens to the rest? It is not spent and by definition in macroeconomics, that means it is saved. This 0.9 is referred to as the marginal propensity to consume (mpc). It is the proportion of a change in income that is spent, or

$$\text{mpc} = \frac{\text{the change of } C}{\text{the change in } Y_d}$$

This is shown in Figure 5.11. But we can see this is the same as the value of the gradient of this line, so we know that the gradient equals the marginal propensity to consume.

Why might this line be important? One reason is that if research using this and more sophisticated techniques shows that the mpc is equal to 0.9, then the consequences of an income tax change can be estimated. For example, reducing tax rates would increase households' disposable income and our results would enable us to estimate that 90 per cent of that increase would be spent and 10 per cent added to savings.

Macroeconomists are not just interested in spending patterns, but

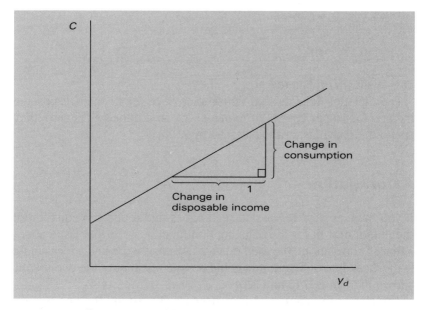

FIGURE 5.11   MARGINAL PROPENSITY TO CONSUME

also in savings. As a first approach, total savings in the economy is defined as that part of current income that is not spent in a particular time period,

savings (S) = disposable income (Y_d) – consumption (C)

gives equation 1:

$$S = Y_d - C$$

It is not a big leap after this to know that if we have identified an equation for C as equation 2:

$$C = 30 + 0.9Y_d$$

we can use this to find the savings equation or as it is often called, the savings function. We simply put the value of C in equation (2) into the equation (1), so

$$S = Y_d - (30 + 0.9Y_d) \text{ and removing the brackets}$$

$$S = Y_d - 30 - 0.9Y_d$$

$$S = 0.1Y_d - 30$$

This is shown on Figure 5.12.

The equation tells us that households save 0.1 of their disposable income (or 10 per cent of it) minus £30m, and if their Y_d is zero, they spend their savings, or they dissave by £30m.

▶ Correlation

If you have applied regression techniques and found the equation of the line of best fit for the consumption function, a further issue arises – that of correlation. The methods we use ensure the line we calculate is the 'best' line of fit, but that could be true of either of the two graphs shown in Figures 5.13 and 5.14.

The cluster in Figure 5.13 is bunched closer round the line than in Figure 5.14, and common sense would tell us that since the scatter looks wilder in Figure 5.14, then the line in Figure 5.14 is in some way different from that in Figure 5.13. We know it is not different in the

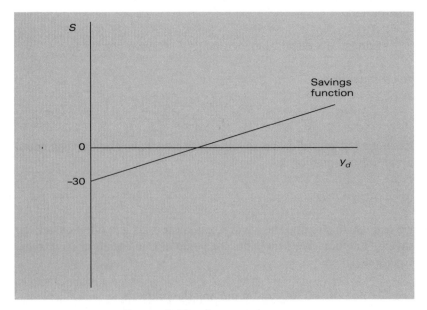

FIGURE 5.12 A SAVINGS FUNCTION

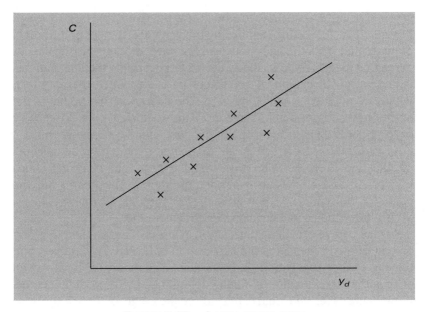

FIGURE 5.13   A HIGH CORRELATION

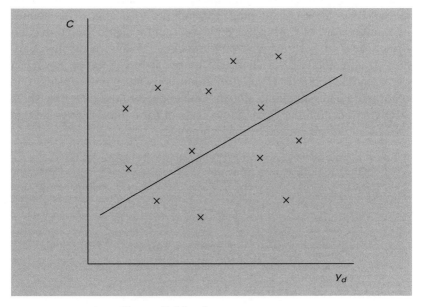

FIGURE 5.14   A LOW CORRELATION

sense of being less accurate in what it sets out to do, that is, go through the middle of the scatter, minimising the vertical distances of the points of the scatter from the line. However, we have another statistical technique that measures how closely the scatter is around the line, and this is known as correlation. A coefficient (r) is calculated that can take values from -1 to $+1$, including zero. The nearer are the points of the scatter to the regression line, the more the coefficient gets closer to $+1$ or to -1 depending on the slope of the line. Figure 5.15 shows this.

If r is equal to $+1$ or -1, then all the points of the scatter actually fall on the line itself. Usually r^2 is calculated so that r^2 takes values between 0 and $+1$, which eases interpretation. The nearer are the points of the scatter to the regression line then the nearer r^2 is to $+1$. Your future studies will develop these ideas further.

So far we have explained correlation in terms of our straight line, and as part of this, r measures the association of these two variables, and this has further applications in economics. The theory we have looked at says that consumption is chiefly determined by disposable income. If this is the case, we would expect to see the points of the scatter close to the line; a wide scatter would indicate that C is moving all over the place, presumably for reasons other than that income is changing. That is, we expect to see our correlation coefficient near $+1$. If we do not then we may doubt our original proposition and look for some other factors that cause consumption expenditure to change. This sounds fine, but a word of warning: even if we found a high correlation coefficient, near to 1, showing strong association between our two variables, the results are very limited. The results mean we do not reject our original proposition, but correlation does not prove causation. In other words, a mathematical technique applied to the data may show strong association between the two sets of data, but it is possible that the variations are caused by something else.

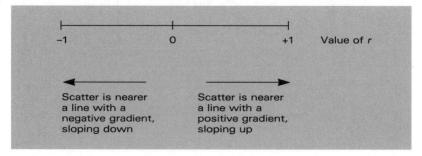

FIGURE 5.15 THE VALUE OF r

For example, in a micro context, when the sales of umbrellas in London stores in summer are relatively high, street vendors' ice-cream sales are relatively low: they are negatively correlated. Does this mean one causes the other? That money spent on ice creams means there is none left for umbrellas, or vice versa? Rather, sales of both are influenced by the weather – that is the main causation factor from a sensible standpoint. So a high correlation between disposable income and consumption may be the result of something else.

Our mathematical techniques are precise and accurate, but the economist must make sense of the economic world and how the techniques may be applied and interpreted in that context. Otherwise they are very limited in their power.

Researchers use more complex and precise methods and will analyse such macro data using non-linear techniques. The ideas looked at can be developed and a larger macro model built using mathematical techniques. In fact a little mathematics goes a long way in macroeconomics, but it is the understanding of the economic phenomena that is paramount.

▶ Index numbers

Another area where numbers and mathematics benefits economists is the use of index numbers. Economists are often attempting to track the performance of data over time. If these data are just total disposable income in the country, this would seem a simple matter, but if the data are being tracked to see how well off we are and whether things are improving or not, the answer is more difficult. Over a run of years, prices may change so that an increase in disposable income of say 2 per cent a year may not mean that consumers can buy more goods and services with the money in their pockets, if prices have risen by a greater annual percentage. There may be other factors involved as well, like changes in the distribution of the total disposable income, or even population changes, although population usually changes only slowly. However, if we focus on the price changes, we have to deal with thousands of prices of the different goods and services purchased, which on the face of it seems a huge task and indeed it is. In practice this is handled by using an index of prices to show how the 'average price' has altered.

If we look at a simple example of a price index it will show us some of the methods involved.

TABLE 5.1 DATA FOR PRICE INDEX

	1998		1999	
	Price	**Expenditure (£)**	**Price**	**Expenditure (£)**
15 litres of petrol	70p/litre	10.50	80p/litre	12.00
3 kilos of potatoes	30p/kilo	.90	40p/kilo	1.20
2 cinema tickets	£4 each	8.00	£4.50 each	9.00
Total expenditure		19.40		22.20

Table 5.1 shows three items and their prices in two years, which we can compare using an index. We do not simply add up the price per unit of each item, but consider a typical weekly combination of quantities bought: in other words a 'basket of shopping' for a particular time period. The cost of this basket in 1998 is £19.40. We then use the same quantities with the new prices for 1999 and find the cost of the same basket of goods in this year: £22.20. If we take 1998 as our basis for comparison, that becomes our base year, and the expenditure for that year is expressed as 100.

Our retail price index for 1999 compares expenditure in that year to that of 1998:

$$\frac{22.20}{19.40} \times \frac{100}{1} = 114.43$$

So the index of these prices is as follows:

1998   100
1999   114.43

This shows that the rate of inflation for this basket of products is 14.43 per cent.

We have taken a basket with only three items. A retail price index includes hundreds of items and many problems arise in its measurement. For instance, do you include everything bought and sold? Which 'average price' do you take? Is it determined by the brand or the retail outlet? How do we get a balance between a jar of coffee, which may last a week, and a car, which may last ten years if driven carefully? How do you deal with new products coming on the market that you could not buy last year? These are just a few of the complications to consider. The study of index numbers looks at these and considers appropriate solutions so that when the index is applied, a reasonably accurate result occurs. But there is no simple solution to some of these questions and there are dangers in ignoring them.

The retail price index attempts to measure and track prices and it has important applications. At the time of writing it is possible to buy National Savings Certificates where the return you receive at maturity date depends partly on the retail price index. These certificates are simply funds lent by the public to the government to finance its activities and the National Debt. There may also be a link made between pay settlements and the retail price index. From these examples we see that indices are important for many people apart from economists analysing the performance of (say) inflation.

We may also make international comparisons using index numbers. This is done in Table 5.2.

The data shows the four countries with consumer price changes broadly in line, with the UK showing the highest changes.

Students of economics at some point will have to consider index numbers, discovering that there are different methods used to calculate them, and many pitfalls in their application, however necessary they may be.

TABLE 5.2   INDICES OF CONSUMER PRICES. ALL ITEMS 1996 = 100

	Denmark	Finland	Sweden	U.K.
1995	98	98.9	99.2	97.6
1996	100	100	100	100
1997	101.9	101.2	101.9	101.8
1998	103.3	102.6	102.9	103.4

Source: *Eurostatistics*, Statistical Office of the European Communities, 12, 1999.

▶ Data issues

In trying to answer economic questions, we often rely on published data. This can create a whole range of issues that students must be aware of and decide how to handle. Let us take an example from published data and examine it.

Family Spending is a publication from the Office for National Statistics (ONS) and provides reports on the annual Family Expenditure Survey. We have taken an extract from one of the tables in the report as follows:

TABLE 5.3   INCOME AND SOURCE OF INCOME BY UK AND GOVERNMENT OFFICE REGIONS 1997–8

(a) Income

	Number of Households	Weekly household income (£)	
		Disposable	Gross
North East	365	285	339
North West and Merseyside	707	328	397
Yorkshire and the Humber	563	299	359
London	658	394	492
South East	1030	409	515
South West	597	347	423

(b) Sources of income as a % of gross weekly household income

	Wages and Salaries	Self Employ-ment	Invest-ment	Annuities and Pensions[1]	Social Security benefits[2]	Other Sources
North East	62	5	4	8	19	1
North West and Merseyside	67	7	4	7	15	1
Yorkshire and the Humber	65	6	4	8	16	2
London	70	9	4	5	10	1
South East	69	9	5	8	9	1
South West	62	11	7	7	12	2

[1] Other than social security benefits.
[2] Excluding housing benefit and council tax benefits.

Source: Family Spending, 1997/8 Office for National Statistics, table 8.7.

This extract gives a regional breakdown of household disposable income, in net and gross figures, and additionally shows the sources of this income in a regional breakdown. Do these data shed any light on regional disparities that may exist? Do they show strong disparities? Is there a north–south divide seen here? To make sense of the data we need to understand the definitions of the terms used by the ONS. What is meant by a household? How are the regions defined? The answers are usually given in the publications where the data appear; for example, in this case, there is a map showing the boundaries of the regions, using the standard classification.

Another issue relating to these data is do we know how they were collected? We are told in the report that 6409 households took part in this survey, and that overall the response rate was 62 per cent, meaning that 38 out of every 100 households asked to participate refused or were unable to do so. Might this have affected the data and introduced some sort of bias into the results? When we look at the number of households in each region, we see they are different. Why is this? Do the numbers reflect the relative sizes of the population in these regions, and/or were the response rates different, or was it something else? The more we know about the data, their definitions and the way they were collected and summarised, then the more confidently we can comment on and use them.

It is also useful to be able to summarise evidence from such tables to highlight the main features. This may involve the use of graphs and charts to show features very clearly, or use relative figures (percentages) to enable clear comparisons to be made. For example, we may calculate the figures given in Table 5.4.

These figures show the disparities clearly: that the weekly disposable income of households in the NE is 69.7 per cent of that of households in the SE.

You may also like to consider what additional light is shed on the issues from the lower part of the table of extracts above. This sort of

TABLE 5.4   WEEKLY DISPOSABLE INCOME AS A % OF THE WEEKLY DISPOSABLE INCOME IN THE SE

NE	NW and Merseyside	Yorks and The Humber	London	SE	SW
69.7	80.2	73.1	96.3	100	84.8

data analysis is common to many disciplines and the techniques involved are often studied in courses where economics is a component. We have tried to show a number of ways in which mathematics and statistics are valuable in the study of economics. Support for further study is available in many texts and their workbooks. We hope you find the techniques you master worth the effort in your economic studies.

Further reading

Jacques, I., (1999) *Mathematics for Economists and Business*, Harlow, Pearson.

Part 2

6 Basic Study Skills

By this time in your academic career, you will have studied for hundreds, perhaps thousands of hours, but that does not mean that you have mastered all the study skills. A professional musician may be at the top of her career, yet still feel the need to improve.

The study skills in this chapter are not exclusive to economics: they are transferable. This means that as you master them, they will be useful in helping you improve in other subjects. As the title suggests, they are basic skills and are easy to absorb. Indeed, much of the advice in this chapter may already be familiar to you, but it is worth reminding yourself of the main things.

First, some principles:

- Learning should be reflective. You need to think about what you are learning; indeed, you should criticise material that you read or are taught.
- Learning should be active. You should approach it with a purpose and some strategies rather than just reading a book.
- Learning should be more concerned with understanding than with memorising. There is a place for learning things off by heart, but in most cases it is far more important to understand than to be able to regurgitate. This is particularly true in economics, which is much more a way of thinking than things to be learned. (though in the early stages there are definitions and concepts that are used in a precise way and which it is useful to remember).
- Ideas and information need to be processed. This means you should think about them, talk about them and write about them.
- Ideas and information need to be reformatted. By this we mean that they need to be transformed to suit your purpose. For example, if you read something in a textbook that is relevant to an essay you are writing, you need to adapt the material so that it helps you develop an argument in your essay.

One final principle before we get down to the nitty gritty. No two people are alike. That means that some of the ideas in this chapter may work very well for most people, but may not be suitable for you. Of course, your lecturers will also offer you help and advice. You need to try out different ideas and adapt them to suit you. One way to do this is to keep a 'learning journal'. This involves noting down and evaluating your studies for a week or so. Note the timing of the study sessions, their place, the content (that is, what you did) and your intentions for the future (that is, what you will do next time). Then, at the end of the week, evaluate each session, recording what was good about it and what was a waste of time. Finally, next time seek to recreate the worthwhile experiences and learn from your mistakes by not repeating the poor sessions. In other words, you should monitor your own efforts.

The folowing sections offer some general advice.

▶ Time and place

Your time is important, and time spent on studying could sometimes be better spent doing other things – remember the concept of opportunity cost? So it is important that you use your time well. This does not mean that you should plan every minute of every day, but there are some useful techniques that can help you find enough time and then use it effectively. It is a good idea to ask for guidance from your tutors as to how much study time they think a particular course needs. This will give you an overview. One of the main differences between school and university is that in higher education you are expected to do much more on your own.

The first thing is to find out what kind of person you are. Do you ever

- Leave things to the last minute?
- Get overloaded so that everything comes all at once?
- Forget things?
- Find that the books you need today are not in the library because someone has taken them out?

If you can answer 'no' to all these questions you are a genius at time management and can skip this section. But if you are a mere mortal, then you will have answered 'yes' to most of the questions. Indeed, it is possible to divide people into two main groups – 'proactors' and 'reactors'. The proactors are always organised, plan ahead and hand work in on time. Reactors are the opposite, always at the last minute, sometimes making the excuse 'I need some pressure before I can do something'. If you are mainly a reactor, then this is for you.

Start by drawing up a chart of a typical week (whilst recognising that every week has some individual characteristics). Table 6.1 gives you an idea of what we mean. Then work out what study time you can reasonably expect to do and fill it in. Similarly, add in your leisure activities and any part-time employment that you may have.

TABLE 6.1 A TYPICAL WEEK'S ACTIVITIES

	Morning	Afternoon	Evening
Sunday			
Monday			
Tuesday			
Wednesday			
Thursday			
Friday			
Saturday			

It is also useful to make a daily plan, perhaps with a layout as shown in Table 6.2. (If you are lucky, you may be able to do this on an electronic organiser.)

When you have done something, tick it off.

TABLE 6.2 AN EXAMPLE OF A DAILY PLAN

Things to be done	Time	Schedule
Cash from bank	08.00	
	09.00	
Hand in essay	10.00	Econ seminar
	11.00	Lecture room 5.3
	12.00	Library
	13.00	Lunch with Pete
Football training	etc.	

Now all of this is a bit perfectionist. No one can always keep to the plans that they have made. And people vary a lot in how they work, so what works for one person may not do so for another. What is important is to have a clear idea of what you need to achieve in the short and long run. So, get organised!

Place is also important. If you are doing something very interesting, then place does not matter very much. You can concentrate anywhere. But unfortunately most academic tasks are not so interesting, so you need to make sure that you study in a place that is conducive to studying. Again, that will vary with the individual: some people insist on loud music when they study whilst others demand absolute quiet. But everyone studies better if they are comfortable – although not too comfortable! In an ideal world you would have a place to yourself, with plenty of room to spread your books, access to a computer, bookshelves, good lighting and a decent filing system. Few people can have all these facilities at their disposal, but students spend many hours studying, so it is worthwhile spending some time getting organised in the first place. A simple thing like having enough files can make a big difference.

▶ Reading

Of course you can read; but can you read *well?* Most of the reading that we do can be characterised as *passive* reading. A good example is reading a newspaper or a light novel for pleasure. It does not matter then if you soon forget what you have read. But reading to learn is very different. We need to remember, but more than that we need to understand and to internalise what we read. By 'internalise' we mean mastering the material so that we can make use of it. And this is very different from reading a newspaper.

Attitudes are important in reading well. If we are reading something interesting that seems very relevant, then it is easy. Unfortunately, we all have to read things that seem boring or irrelevant. This is a difficult problem since you cannot learn effectively unless you become interested in what you are reading. One hint is to ask yourself why other people have found this interesting. Presumably the author has; and if the material is recommended reading from your tutor, then your tutor thought it worthwhile. So, try to take on the attitudes of those who did think the material was interesting. Then, ask questions – it is questions that make something interesting. When you find something boring, it may be because you cannot see what the author is getting at. Skim around the book and ask yourself some questions, such as 'Why is this important?' or 'How does this affect economic policy?' Then go back to you reading with a clearer focus.

Of course, this procedure is not infallible; what you are reading may still be boring. One reason for this may be the language used by the author. Sometimes, this is inevitable since the material may be technical, requiring the use of jargon. Economics is full of jargon, with words having a precise and specialised meaning. 'Demand' is an example. This is a word we use carelessly in everyday life, but in economics it has a special meaning as we have seen (p. 16). Jargon can put you off at first, but when you have mastered it, jargon can lead to precise meanings and concise expression. A dictionary can be useful here, but note that an ordinary English dictionary may not be very useful since economics has a specialised language. Many textbooks now include a glossary that can help you with this problem, but there are a number of good economics dictionaries on the market. If you are thinking of studying quite a bit of economics, it is a good idea to buy one of these. In the meantime, the index to this book will help you refer to some common terms. Another approach is to write down the difficult words you come across, together with a reference. This will help when you meet the word again.

Another reason why you might find academic writing off-putting is that it is written in an impersonal style, in the third person passive: 'It is sometimes found', or 'It can be concluded that'. This is in contrast with non-academic writing which is usually direct and personal in style. (You may have noticed that we have tried to make this book more interesting by using a more personal approach.) However, cautious language is inevitable in academic writing. That is because academic authors have to be as exact as possible. One difference between social science and everyday writing is the need for precision; in this context, half-truths are no truths. This requirement means that sentences have to be qualified, and the underlying assumptions made clear. So, a journalist may write, 'People in Liverpool are poorer than those in London'. An economist may write 'Research by XYZ suggests that the mean income of households in Liverpool in 1999 was significantly lower than those in London'. As you see, the journalist's version is much easier to read; the economist's more precise.

Sometimes, when you are reading difficult material, you will get stuck. If you are very conscientious you may try to keep looking at the same page – a sure recipe for boredom. Instead, try casting around for clues. Look back to the beginning of the chapter and ask, 'What is the author about?' Or look to the end of the section; often you will find a summary or conclusion that will give you clues. Reread the book's introduction since this often gives a good summary of the author's aims. Another hint is to jot down a few main points – not long notes but a sentence for each paragraph. Also, it is often a good idea to try another book on the same subject. One author's style may not suit you. Changing books may give you new insights. If all these fail – ask. Often another student may have understood the piece and be willing to help, or ask your tutor. Unless it is at an inconvenient time, tutors usually welcome queries from students. Learning should be a collaborative activity, so in turn be willing to help other students.

Reading complex tables is difficult for many students. They see lots of numbers and cannot find their way round them. So, here are a few hints, using Table 6.3 as an example.

First, the obvious – find out what the table is about. In other words, read the title. This should give you an indication of the contents, and also what is not covered. In Table 6.3, the figures are *estimates*, so cannot be regarded as precise. And many European countries are not included. Then look at the date. International statistics are always delayed since they depend on the slowest country reporting. Ask yourself if there have been any major changes since then.

TABLE 6.3 ESTIMATED HOUSING TENURE AND GDP PER CAPITA IN SELECTED WESTERN EUROPEAN COUNTRIES, 1994

	GDP per capita (US$)	Owner-occupation (%)	Private rented (%)	Social rented (%)	Other tenure (%)
Ireland	15 100	80	9	11	–
Spain	12 500	76	16	2	6
Italy	18 400	67	8	6	19
UK	18 950	66	10	24	–
France	23 550	54	21	17	8
Netherlands	21 300	47	17	36	–
Sweden	23 270	43	16	22	19
Germany	26 000	38	36	26	–
Switzerland	36 430	31	60	3	6

Source: European Liaison Committee for Social Housing (1995), Economist Publications, quoted in Atkinson, B., Livesey, F. and Milward, B., *Applied Economics*, Macmillan, p. 179.

Next, look at the source – who says so? If you have statistics about pollution published by the chemical industry, they may be accurate, but they may not be unbiased – for example, they may exclude undesirable elements. In this case the source seems as if it may be authoritative; at least it seems to be official. Then look at the main features. In some tables, you will find totals, and that would be a good starting point. However, in this example we have two types of statistics, some for GDP per capita, and some percentages. The GDP figures have been used to order the table, with one exception – for some reason, Ireland and Spain are in the wrong order. Also note that these are GDP statistics, and therefore have considerable limitations. So far as tenure is concerned, what are the main features? Answer: in almost all countries, owner-occupation is by far the most common form of tenure. Again, there is an anomaly – the two richest countries have the lowest proportion of people owning their own house. If we were investigating this topic, we would want to know why, since in the UK we expect better off people to own their own home.

So, to summarise the procedures for examining tables:

* Examine the title
* Examine the source
* Look at the main features, for example, the main trends . You can do this by looking across and down the table
* Ask questions about the table

Speed of reading is another factor to be considered. We need to vary the speed at which we read, depending on our purpose. In particular, reading speed will depend on various factors such as how much you know already about the subject, on the difficulty of the book, and how thoroughly you need to understand it. When the text is easy and the material familiar, you may read about 100 words a minute. On the

TABLE 6.4 VARYING YOUR READING RATES

Your purpose	Technique
Trial reading	Quick survey
Search for particular word or example	Scanning
Quick overview	Skimming
Understand main ideas	Fast reading
Critical reading	Slow, critical reading

other hand, when you need to master difficult material, 40 words a minute may be good progress.

Let us look at each of these in turn. By 'trial reading' I mean taking a quick look at the contents of a book, probably in the library, to see if it will be useful. In this case a quick survey of the contents, chapter headings, introduction and conclusion may be enough. This will only take a few minutes, even for quite a large book.

Sometimes you will need to scan a text. This is the technique to use when you want an example to illustrate a point, or to find a particular concept. In this case, you may only need to use the index, or flip through a few pages, looking for the point you want.

Skimming is a very useful technique. This is used to get an overall idea of what is in the text. It is useful to do this frequently, particularly at the beginning of a chapter. That is because if you have some idea of what is coming when you read more carefully, you will understand the material better since it will have a context. Skimming is a rather quicker version of what I called 'fast reading' in the table. This is used when the material is easy and you only want a general overview of the main points. This contrasts with 'critical reading' which is inevitably slow, but which should give you mastery of material, if you approach it properly.

In order to do this you need to read *actively* in order to remember what you have read. And the best way to do this is to make notes.

▶ Note-taking

We will discuss taking notes in lectures in the next section; here we are just concerned with taking notes when reading.

There is a skill in taking good notes, but many students are very poor at this. The main factor to consider is your time, which is valuable. Some students spend many hours on this task and their notes end up nearly as long as the original. If you do own the book or have a photocopy, then it is a good idea to highlight the main points (*never* do this in a library book). Alternatively, you can underline the main points in pencil. Before starting, ask yourself why you are highlighting. Often, this will be to focus your attention on the main points you are going to incorporate in an essay or presentation. At other times, you will be pointing out ideas that you will want to remember, for example, because the topic may come up in an exam. In this case, you will need to supplement your highlighting with *brief* notes – there is no point spending a great deal of time on a task if it is not needed. This reinforces what you have read, and will also point you to the main areas you have highlighted when you come to revise.

Good notes are essential if you really want to master a text. That is because note-taking forces you to think about what you are reading. Good notes should pick out the main points that the author is making. One hint in doing this is to look at the author's summary or the last paragraph in a chapter since this will often sum up the writer's thoughts. Also, it is often helpful if you write down your thoughts about what you read. For example, you could give your own examples, or extend the argument or else suggest where the argument is weak. Sometimes it is worth while noting down little quotations or statistics that might be useful later on.

There are three main ways of making notes. One is to write a brief summary, but in your own words. An alternative is to make lists of the main points. The third way is to illustrate the ideas in the text. Figure 6.1 gives an (incomplete) example of how someone might summarise diagrammatically an article about poverty in the UK. The method you choose will depend partly on the text; for example, some topics are difficult to convert into a diagram. It will also depend on how you think – some people find it easier to think in visual terms.

It is a good idea to give your own examples in your notes to illustrate the points being made. If you keep your wits about you, you will find many examples in everyday life. Follow the economic news in the media. If you get a newspaper, then cut out articles that feature economic events and file these in an appropriate place in your notes.

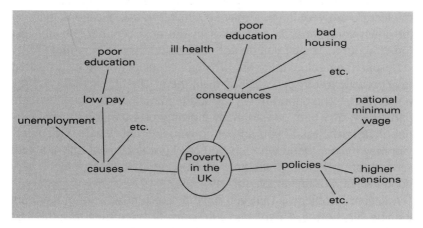

FIGURE 6.1   A SAMPLE DIAGRAM

When you come to revise, you will find it useful if you have collated your notes from various sources so that lecture notes, photocopies and newspaper cuttings relating to a particular topic are all together.

One thing you must do when writing notes is to give a full reference to the source. This is discussed in more detail in the chapter on writing essays. Here I will just give the principle: your references should be detailed enough to let you – and any reader – find the original (including the page).

One final point about your notes. All too often students spend a lot of time writing notes, then put them away and never look at them again. To avoid this, you need to develop an efficient system of filing the notes you make. This may involve a different file for each subject that you take.

▶ Lectures

Many people – including lecturers – are sometimes cynical about the use of lectures because they encourage rote learning. But that is not always the case: lectures do offer a good way of learning. First, they offer a way of presenting information. They can also make students think by showing how the ideas in the subject can be used. They can offer a kind of map, showing the territory to be covered and the main features to look out for and which you can follow up in your own studies. Good lecturers can help you master an argument that may be difficult in a textbook. In order to help lecturers to do this, it is important that if you do not understand, you ask questions. If the numbers in the lecture are very large, it may be difficult to ask questions then, so jot down your question and ask it in the next seminar. Do not just forget about it. The bit you do not understand may be very important.

Despite their value, there are problems associated with lectures that may prevent you from benefiting from them. The first is that you may not be there. The opportunity cost of attending a lecture may be high, particularly at 9 a.m. on a Monday morning or 4 p.m. on Friday afternoon! Nevertheless, if you do not go, you will not benefit. Of course, you may have a friend who lets you copy her notes, but this is a very second-rate solution. Notes are personal, and her notes may be very good for her, but unsuitable for you.

A second problem is that you have to concentrate; some lecturers may be very boring. There is no sure way of overcoming this; the best is to keep asking questions of yourself – 'What is this about? Why is it important?' You need to be prepared to work at lectures. It may seem to be a reactive process, but you need to make it proactive.The third problem is that you have to take notes. This can be difficult; sometimes students are so busy writing that they stop thinking. So, begin by asking why you are making notes. Some courses are built round lectures; there may be few relevant books or other materials. In such cases, you may need to make long and detailed notes of what the lecturer says. This will probably be the case in quantitative courses. However, most economics courses are not like that, though this may be the case for a specialised option in the later years of a degree course. So, keep your notes brief and to the point. This means thinking before you write. In most cases, if you get the main thrust, you will be able to fill out your notes from a textbook. What you should write are the main headings and also examples that you may not be able to find in books. Also, write down the names of major writers and summarise their theories of their research findings.

One technique that helps solve the problem of finding time to write in a lecture is to use abbreviations. Some of these are obvious and well-known, for example, 'e.g.' for example, 'no.' for number, or '£' for pounds. In addition you may invent your own. This can be useful if you are consistent, but be careful – there are few things more frustrating than finding you cannot understand the abbreviations you used a few months ago. Sometimes people find it useful to summarise lectures by using diagrams along the lines of Figure 6.1 above.

Your time after the lecture is also important. In an ideal world, you would find time to write a neat summary of the lecture. But we do not live in an ideal world. Nevertheless, it is worthwhile looking at your notes just after the lecture whilst it is fresh in your mind and making sure that they are clear – will you be able to understand them in a few weeks' time? And try discussing lecture content with your friends.

▶ Seminars and tutorials

In this book, we will use these two words interchangeably to mean a learning session where (relatively) small numbers of students meet with a tutor to discuss particular aspects of a course.

Why do we have discussion groups? One is that they give students a chance to ask questions that shyness or large numbers may prevent them asking in lectures. So, if there are aspects of the topic that you are uncertain about, jot down your questions before you go. Tutors often arrive early, and this gives you an opportunity to ask informally. If this is not possible, then ask in the tutorial. Lecturers usually welcome questions – it shows that you are thinking about the subject. There are other reasons why seminars and tutorials are useful:

* To integrate learning from lectures and reading
* To clarify your ideas – talking about a topic is a good way to do this
* To practise communication with others – this is an important job skill, much desired by employers
* To increase the opportunities for students to help each other. Tutorials are a good way to get to know other students taking your course and to learn from them – or to help them. Teaching is a good way of learning!

In order to get the best out of a tutorial you will need to prepare for it. At the beginning of term tutors will often give out a list of topics to be discussed. This means that a day or two before the seminar you have a chance to look through your notes or a relevant book and get organised. For example, list things you do not understand, then the main points that you think might arise and questions that this might throw up. For example, if the topic is the economic effects of trade unions, you might jot down the possible advantages and disadvantages and think about what this might mean for government policy towards trade unions.

Many students do find discussion difficult – they think that the others will all know more about the topic than they do. Now, there is nothing wrong in sitting quietly and listening, but you will gain much more if you do take an active part. Stop worrying about what others are thinking about you – they are probably worrying about what *you* are thinking about them.

Sometimes you may have to give a presentation. This is the word used to describe the situation where one or more students have to report back to the group the results of some work that they have done. Sometimes this is very informal, but sometimes presentations can be an assessed piece of work requiring much preparation. This requires you to think about two things – what you are going to say, and how you are going to say it.

What you say will largely be determined by the topic. You will often have a time limit, so practise before the presentation to check that it is the right length. Try to emphasise the main points that you want to get over, for example, by highlighting them in your notes. Also make sure that you have kept full references for any material that you have taken from books or articles. Another hint is to persuade a friend to listen to what you are going to say and to make suggestions.

In considering your delivery, there are a number of things to bear in mind. The first is obvious – get there on time, or preferably early if you are going to use some visual aids: there are few things more embarrassing than hoping to make extensive use of (say) an overhead projector and then finding that there is not one in the room or that it does not work. Try to face your audience, so do not talk at the same time that you are writing on the board. Look people in the eye as you talk – just as you would in conversation with them. And try not to read your script too quickly.

There are two things in particular that you can do after a seminar to improve its learning value. The first is to jot down the main things that you have learned and to file them away properly. The other is to talk about the topic with your friends. Learn from them as well as from your tutors.

▶ Conclusion

This chapter may read like a counsel of perfection. What we have tried to do is to give a large number of hints to improve your learning. No one will adopt them all. You must choose what is useful and practical for you. The most important thing to remember is that your learning should be active. Do not be like a sponge, just letting things soak in; rather be like a squirrel, seeking out useful things, storing them and making use of them when appropriate.

Further reading

Cottrell, S. (1999) *The Study Skills Handbook,* Basingstoke, Macmillan.
Northedge, A. (1990) *The Good Study Guide*, Milton Keynes, Open University Press.
Saunders, D. (1994) *The Complete Student Handbook*, Oxford, Blackwell.

7 Writing Economics Essays

▶ What's the point of essays?

It is not by chance that essay writing is so prevalent in higher education. The reason is that it serves several functions. Here we will just mention four:

1. In the first place, it is a convenient way of assessing students' knowledge and skills in many subject areas; hence if you master the techniques of writing economics essays, with only a little variation you will be able to write good essays in other subjects. That is because economics essays require skills such as the ability to organise knowledge and to write clearly.
2. From the student's point of view they are a good way to internalise knowledge. That is because they make you think about the topic and organise your thoughts. This is a good way to really understand.
3. Next they help you develop the capacity for rational argument. This is particularly important in economics where students have to assess the strengths and weaknesses of competing approaches, for example, assessing the appropriateness of a government's competition policy.
4. A fourth function of essay writing is that it generates feedback. In secondary school, pupils often have to complete pieces of work very frequently; with age the frequency diminishes and in higher education you may only have one or two pieces of work a term. So, you may not know how you are doing until you have to write an essay.

▶ What makes a good essay?

A fundamental aspect of a good essay is that it answers the actual question asked. That may seem obvious, but a very common fault of student essays is that they just write generally about the topic rather than focusing on the specific question. One way to check if you have answered the question is to read out your answer to a friend and ask her to guess the question. If she cannot, then you need to think again. Table 7.1 lists some of the criteria use by the Open University for evaluating essays. You can use it to try and evaluate your own work – a very good thing to do.

Preparation

No student can just sit down and write a good essay; preparation is essential. This should begin by reviewing any earlier essays that you have written. What was good about them? What was not so good? Did your tutor make any comments that you could use to improve the essay you are about to start?

The next step, and perhaps the most important of all, is to read the question and to think about what it means. You will have seen in Table 7.1 that a crucial feature of a good essay is that the material in a good answer is relevant; that you answer the actual question. So, begin by looking at the question several days before you get down to serious work on it. This will let you digest what it is really about. Moreover, you may come across material that will be useful while you are doing something else such as reading the paper – a good example of serendipity.

There are often key words in a question; some of these are explained in Table 7.2.

Once you have understood the directive words such as assess, you need to make sure you understand the economic aspects of the question. Three ideas can help you here:

1. Make sure you understand the concepts in the question. Dictionaries of economics are useful here; also, many textbooks have glossaries.
2. Rewrite the question in your own words. Then make sure that you understand what it really means.
3. Brainstorm round the topic. Jot down any ideas which come into your head. The idea behind brainstorming is that one idea can lead to another, so generating other ideas. Many of these may prove to be irrelevant, but some should be useful. It is often useful to brainstorm with a friend – you can stimulate each other. The ideas that you generate can give you ideas for a library search.

TABLE 7.1 CRITERIA FOR EVALUATING SOCIAL SCIENCE ESSAYS

An excellent pass

- demonstrate comprehensive coverage of an area
- include critical evaluation
- demonstrate the ability to integrate a range of materials
- provide full references

A good pass

- be generally accurate and well informed
- be well organised and structured
- address the question
- show an ability to evaluate the material

A clear pass

- be generally accurate, though with some omissions and errors
- be expressed in the author's own words
- define key terms
- show an understanding, but no real development of the arguments

A bare pass

- answer the question only tangentially
- fail to support argument with adequate evidence
- show only sparse coverage of relevant material
- miss a key point of information

A bare fail

- fail to answer the question directly
- contain little appropriate material
- be plagiarised (sometimes)
- lack any real argument

A clear fail

- * show a profound misunderstanding of basic material
- * fail to understand or answer the question
- * be plagiarised
- be incoherent

Source: Extract from Redman, P. *et al.* (1998) *Good Essay Writing*, Milton Keynes, Open University.

TABLE 7.2 KEY WORDS IN ESSAYS

Account for	Give reasons for (as opposed to 'give an account of' which just requires a description)
Analyse	Examine critically
Assess	Use evidence to evaluate an argument or determine the value of
Compare	Look for similarities and differences between two approaches; perhaps give more weight to similarities
Contrast	Bring out the differences between two approaches
Criticise	Assess the strengths and weaknesses of a statement or idea
Define	Give the precise meaning of a concept or phrase
Describe	Give an account of
Discuss	Define the main terms and develop logical arguments
Evaluate	Similar to 'assess': evaluate theories or arguments
Explain	Explain the reasons why
How far	Assess the truth of a statement
Illustrate	Give examples
Review	Survey a topic and evaluate it
Outline	Describe the main features briefly
Summarise	See 'outline'

Source: *Good Essay Writing. A Social Sciences Guide*, Milton Keynes, Open University, adapted from material in Redman, P. *et al.*, op cit p. 66, and Purvis, R. 'Writing Essays', in Saunders, D. (ed.) (1994) *The Complete Student Handbook*, Oxford, Blackwell, p. 143.

Searching for material is discussed in detail in Chapter 9 which deals with writing dissertations. This includes using the Internet, which may be useful in writing essays, so you may care to look at this part of that chapter now. Moreover, many institutions may use intranet facilities to make material available to students; check if this applies to you. Here we want just to mention one or two points. The first, and most important, is that your greatest help in finding things out is a librarian. Pressures on public spending mean that they may not have time to do all that they would like, but they are the experts. If you want to find out how big UK exports were in the year 2000, or how many people work in the car industry, then a librarian in a good library will point you to a likely source.

However, there is a good deal that you can do to help yourself. When you are writing an essay your time is limited; you are not expected to find out all that there is to know on a topic. For most essays in the first year of higher education a couple of textbooks and perhaps a couple of specialist books will give you plenty of material (though to this you may need to add some recent statistics). So, the first thing you need to know is the organisation of your library.

Most libraries in the UK are organised on the lines suggested by an American called Melvil Dewey in the nineteenth century. This has one big advantage, and one disadvantage. The advantage means that you can often go to other libraries and easily find out what you want; the disadvantage is that because it originated so long ago, recent developments are difficult to fit in – this is a particular problem in science. Hence some libraries use other systems.

The Dewey system begins by organising all knowledge into ten main categories such as Religion, Social Sciences, Languages and Arts. These are then numbered and the areas are then further subdivided, so that the 300s – the Social Sciences – are split up into areas such as 310 Statistics, 320 Political Science, 330 Economics, 340 Law, and so on. This means that in a library using the Dewey system, books on economics will be numbered in the 330s, though some on trade will be in the 380s.

Then there is another subdivision, so that economics is subdivided:

330   General economics
331   Labour economics
332   Financial
333   Land economics
334   Co-operatives
335   Socialism
336   Public finance
337   International
338   Production
339   Macroeconomics

These are further subdivided, so that 336, for example, is split up:

366.1   Revenues

336.2   Tax
336.3   Public securities, debt
336.4   Public finance of specified countries
etc

Finally, even these numbers are further subdivided, for example, to separate material from different countries.

A couple of examples will illustrate the system. Almost all introductory economics books will be shelved under the number 330. This is therefore the first place you should look if you want a general introduction to the subject. If you want a specialist book on, say, labour economics, then this will be filed under 331. Numbers after the decimal point often refer to specific countries, so that a book on UK tax would have a slightly different number than one on tax in the USA. The big advantage of this from a student's point of view is that a quick look at the shelves will often show you what books are available.

A word of warning. If you are given several weeks to prepare an essay, it is no use waiting until a day or two before, and then going to the library. You will probably find that the books you want are out. So go to the library as soon as you know the titles of your essays and reserve the books you will need. If you get there early, you can write the essay early- it takes no longer to write an essay a month in advance than it does a day before it is due.

Two strategies can alleviate, though not eliminate, the book problem. The first is that you should buy books recommended by your tutor. Students' financial problems mean that this is often difficult. Sometimes you can co-operate with a friend on the same courses, so that you buy book A and he buys book B. Then you can borrow each other's books. If you do not have all the material you need to actually write the essay, you can often make appropriate notes or photocopy particularly useful pages so that you have material when you come to the writing stage. If you do this, make sure that you note down full references.

▶ Types of essay

There are different types of essays in economics and each type requires rather different strategies if you are to do well. Note, however, that sometimes these types overlap, especially in two-part essays where the first part may require you to describe something and the second is more analytical. For example, consider a question such as 'Describe the work of the European Central Bank. Do you think its policy decisions have benefited the European economies?' The first part is quite straightforward – assuming that you can find material on the work of the Bank. The second part requires much greater academic skills.

As this question suggests, some essays require a descriptive approach. These are relatively uncommon at higher levels. They are relatively easy to do at a low level, but difficult to develop to a high standard since they often end up becoming mere summaries. A typical question might be 'Describe the economic policy of the Labour government elected in 1997'. The most important thing to do in answering this question is to get a good plan. One approach would be to answer the question chronologically. Hence a simple plan might be:

1. Introduction – the economic situation on its election
2. The first budget (summarise the main points)
3. Economic policy in the middle years
4. Recent economic policy
5. Conclusion

The advantage of this is that it is very straightforward, if a little uninspiring. An alternative, more enterprising approach would be to choose various themes:

1. Introduction – the economic situation at the time of the election
2. Policy towards employment: welfare to work
3. Inflation policy
4. Competition policy
   Etc.
   Conclusion – common themes

This kind of structure would enable you to comment on the policies under each section. One difficulty is that some policies might not fit easily into only one policy area. For example, an increase in tax on fuel might be discussed in a paragraph on environmental policy, but it would also impact on transport and inflation. Moreover, this approach requires more planning since you have to sort out and organise a range of economic policies into a coherent structure before you can start writing. So, this approach is likely to lead to higher grades if done well, but requires more thought.

Another type of question focuses on explanation. Such a question might be 'Explain the monetarist approach to inflation', or 'What factors explain the distribution of incomes in the UK?' These kinds of questions require you to do more than describe. To give a good answer, you have to discriminate as well as organise. For example, a question asking 'What factors . . . ?' forces you to decide for yourself which things are important and which are not. Then you can divide the subject matter into various categories and give a paragraph to each category. A very similar pattern is required when you answer a 'causal' question such as 'What were the causes of the great depression of the 1930s?' A possible structure for an answer to this question might be:

1. Introduction – brief account of the main features of the depression
2. National causes
   (a) Government policy
       (i) Keynesian critique
       (ii) Monetary policy
   (b) Failure of firms – lack of investment
3. International causes
   (a) Decline in world trade
   (b) Effect of events in USA
4. Conclusion – evaluation of the various causes

(Note that this plan, like the others here, is meant to indicate an approach, rather than give a full answer.)

In questions such as this, various approaches are possible; the essential step to take before writing is to get the material organised in your mind. Then work out a plan that suits your approach. For example, you might decide that the national – international approach just outlined was not suitable. In this case you could structure your essay round an alternative such as first discussing fundamental/long -term causes and then the short-term/immediate factors. Deciding your approach and developing a plan is often the most difficult stage of essay writing. If you get it right, the essay should flow.

These kinds of question are useful because they make you internalise the knowledge. You have to think about the question before you answer, and this leads to greater understanding. The essential thing is that you need to organise the material in a structured way. In this type of essay, as in others, it greatly strengthens your answer if you can give relevant examples to illustrate your argument. That is why it is particularly useful to keep up to date with economic news and events.

A final type of question requires you to evaluate. 'Should Britain join the European Single currency?' is an example. 'Is the public sector too large?' is another. In microeconomics you might be asked to answer questions such as 'Evaluate the government's competition policy'. These evaluation questions require higher academic skills, and can therefore be very challenging. They require you to explore arguments for and against a particular position and also to assess their strengths and weaknesses. A typical plan for such an essay might be:

1. Introduction – describe the present position
2. Give the arguments for a particular approach
3. Give the arguments against
5. Assess the arguments

Alternatively, you could assess and evaluate the arguments as you give them. For example, in an essay on the advantages and disadvantages of Britain joining the European single currency, you could say that one advantage would be that it would eliminate the transactions costs which occur when money has to be changed. Then you could assess this argument – is it a strong one? Are these costs large or small? After a paragraph on this, you then go on to give another argument in favour of UK membership and evaluate this. Then repeat the procedure for the possible disadvantages. At the end of your essay, you come to a conclusion as to which argument is the stronger.

A variation of the evaluation type of question is the 'compare and contrast' question, such as 'Compare and contrast the Keynesian and monetarist approaches to running the economy'. Here, you need not only to describe the essentials of each approach, but also to get a good grade, you need to analyse and evaluate. For example, you need to discuss the assumptions underlying the two approaches and to point out the strengths and weaknesses of the two theories.

Whatever the type of essay, the essential feature is that you need to think before writing.

▶ The structure of an essay

Let us state the obvious. An essay should have a beginning, a middle and an end; more usefully, it should have an introduction, a main or development section, and a conclusion. The introduction is often the most difficult. Once you have got the essay under way, it is relatively easy to continue, but how to get started? One way to begin is to say what you intend to do in your essay. For example, 'In this essay I will begin by describing the case for Britain joining the single currency. Then I will . . . '. In other words, you begin by signposting the material in the rest of the essay. This gets you going, it alerts the reader to what follows and it gives your essay a structure to follow (though some tutors may think that this approach is a bit obvious).

An alternative method of writing an introduction is to begin by defining and explaining the main terms. For example, if you were writing an essay about the advantages and disadvantages of monetarism, you could begin by defining monetarism: 'In this essay "monetarism" will be taken to mean . . . '. A variation of this approach is to begin by explaining the question. For example, the answer to a question about economic development will depend on what you mean by 'development' and you could begin by explaining your approach. Does it just mean increases in national output, or does 'development' mean something broader, perhaps including something about human development? In your introduction you can also state what you are including (or excluding) and also explain your methodology.

One final point about introductions – you should not make them too long. Aim for a crisp, clear start. As a general rule a very full introduction should not exceed 10 per cent of your essay, and if possible should only be about 5 per cent or even less. In short essays, and particularly in examinations, it can be cut to just one or two sentences. Examinations are discussed in Chapter 8.

The main part of your essay needs to have a logical progression, in other words to be sequenced. In order to do this effectively, you need to plan all the main points in your essay. One technique is to write a brief note setting out the main point of each paragraph, then put these into sequence, making sure that there is a good reason why paragraph 2 follows paragraph 1 and so on. Your aim should be to develop an argument, and the suggested structures for various kinds of essay discussed in the previous section should help you achieve this.

In addition, each point in your argument should be supported by evidence. Sometimes, this will be in the form of examples. For example, in an essay about the pricing policy of privatised industries, you may include specific examples of pricing changes. Sometimes two examples from different sources will emphasise important points. Other kinds of evidence might include empirical data. 'Data' in this context do not just mean statistical evidence; they can also be written material. A typical example might be a summary of someone's research. Thus in an essay about low pay, you might have a sentence: 'Research into wages in the catering industry by XYZ showed that . . .'. Often government statistics are a good source of evidence and can be used to support an argument. But it is not enough just to quote evidence; you need to be critical of your sources. For example, in quoting research, you may point out that the data are now dated, or that the sample was small or unrepresentative.

The conclusion of an essay is important because it will be the last thing your tutor reads before it is assessed. The main function of a conclusion is to provide a condensed version of the central arguments and to refer back to the specific question. Now, you should know these before you start, and one very useful idea is that you should approach an essay as you would a journey; you need to know where you are going before you set off, otherwise you will wander round and round, going nowhere in particular. Hence, a useful suggestion is to write the main sentence of your conclusion before you start writing; this is your destination. Then all that you write should lead up to this conclusion, just as every mile on a journey should lead to the destination. For example, if you are writing an essay on the government's competition policy, your reading may have convinced you that it is seriously inadequate. So, write down 'The evidence is clear: the government's competition policy is inadequate.' This will form the lead sentence in your conclusion, and all that you will write in your essay will lead up to this conclusion, though, of course, you will need to consider counter arguments before reaching this final verdict. Similarly, reading for an essay on taxation policy may have led you to the conclusion that taxes should be raised (or cut). Before you start writing, put down your conclusion: 'The conclusion is clear; the government should raise (cut) taxes.' Then, as before, the points in your essay should lead inexorably to this conclusion. Of course, in some cases you may judge that the argument is finely balanced, and your conclusion should reflect this.

The conclusion, like the introduction, should not normally exceed 10 per cent of your essay. It should recap the main points in your argument, and focus very specifically on the question. One way to check that it does this is to see if it contains many of the key words in the question. If it does not, you may have wandered away from the topic. Often it is useful to point out the limitations of your analysis. For example, in an essay about taxation, you may point out that you have focused mainly on income tax and largely ignored other taxes.

Similarly, in an essay on privatisation, you may emphasise that space considerations have led you to concentrate on two or three industries. In some cases you may need to point out that the statistics that you have used are dated or have other limitations, such as not measuring precisely what you want. For example, in an essay on housing, you may need to use statistics on overcrowding as a proxy for 'poor'. One thing that a conclusion should *not* do is to introduce new points. These detract from the central thrust of the argument.

▶ References

When writing an academic essay it is inevitable that you will draw on the work of others. Moreover, one of the characteristics of a good essay is that you show that you have done some reading and know what has been written in the area. In both these cases you need to acknowledge your sources. There is another reason for giving references: they enable others who read what you have written a chance to follow up the ideas you have discussed. This will not often be the case for an essay, but it is quite common for dissertations and books, and giving proper references in an essay is good practice.

So, what should be referenced? All quotations (that is, when you use the actual words of someone else) must be acknowledged. 'Quotations' in this context also includes statistical material. You should also give references when you have paraphrased an author. For example, if you are summarising another writer's ideas, you should acknowledge this. You should also give references when you refer to particular pieces of research. If in doubt, err on the cautious side and give a reference. Finally, you should give references when you give facts that are not generally known. For example, you would need to give a source if you wrote that 'unemployment in the UK in January 2000 was x million'. Similarly, you would give a reference for a sentence such as 'Since privatisation, prices in the water industry have risen by x per cent.' Since it is generally known, you would not need to give a reference if you wrote 'Tony Blair became Prime Minister in 1997.'

The basic principle of giving a reference is that it should enable a reader to go directly to the original source. There are two main ways of doing this. One is to list the references as you go along by putting a number such as (1) after the quotation or other material. You then elaborate this at the end of your essay. However, the most common system of referencing is called the Harvard system.

The basic idea of this system is that immediately after giving a quotation you give the author's name, the date of publication and the page number. The date is given because the same author may have written several books, or there may be different editions of the book you have used. Giving the page number means that a reader can go straight to the original source. For example, if you were giving a reference to the sentence you are now reading, you would write (Atkinson and Johns, 2001, p. 142). The full stop comes after the bracket. If you are summarising several pages, you can put 'ff' after the page number to signify 'following'.

At the end of your essay, you then elaborate this under a heading 'References'. A good reference will be in the order:

- author's surname (when there are several you should list them all)
- the date of publication of the edition you have used
- the book's title
- the place of publication and the publisher

For example, if you were referencing this book, you would write: 'Atkinson, B. and Johns, S. (2001) *Studying Economics*, Basingstoke, Palgrave.'

That is relatively straightforward, but there are sometimes complications. When there are three or more authors, it is acceptable not to list them all in the text, but just to list the first author and then put '*et al.*' (this means 'and others'). When you give the full reference at the end, you should list all the authors, though common sense can prevail if there are many authors. For example, the book I have listed as Redman *et al.* lists thirteen members of a project team as the authors: clearly too many to list.

When you are quoting an author in a book edited by someone else, you should give the actual author's name in the text, and in the reference at the end, give the editor's name. For example, if the author was Smith and the editor Jones, your text reference would be (Smith, 1999, p. 17) and reference at the end would be: 'Smith, J. (1999) 'How to give references' in Jones, B. (ed.)' – then give the book's title in italics and then the place and publisher in ordinary type. (If you are not using a computer for your essay, just underline where you would use italics.)

A similar principle applies when you are quoting an article from a journal. In this case the journal title would be given in italics. You would also give the volume number and the first and last pages of the article, so the end of the reference would read '*Economics*, vol. 23, no. 2, pp. 17–25. (Note that these are examples, not actual references.)

Much of this is conventional; the underlying principle is that a reader must be able to go directly to the original source. A good reference will make this possible, a bad one will not. Note also that different institutions sometimes have different styles.

One final and important point about references. When making notes you should always write down the source as you go along. There are few things so frustrating as writing an essay and then realising that you are not certain of the source of your note or photocopy.

▶ Style

An essay should be in your own words – unless you acknowledge the source. If you do not do this, it is plagiarism. It is often very tempting to use other people's words because it is easy and they can write better than you can. But copying other people's work is cheating. This also applies even if you make minor changes to the original. The penalty is a failed grade.

The first step in avoiding plagiarism is to be aware of the problem and to make a conscious decision not to copy. The second way is to master the ideas in your head before writing, then close your books and write your own thoughts. Finally, if there is any doubt, give a reference. In any case, using your own words leads to better learning; expressing ideas for yourself forces you to understand what you are writing.

It is usually good academic practice to use an objective style. Earlier in this chapter, we suggested that one way to begin an essay was to write 'In this essay I will . . . '. That would not be regarded as good practice by some academics; they would prefer an impersonal approach such as 'This essay will . . . '. The reason for avoiding the 'I' word is that it sometimes suggests a lack of objectivity, and economists are supposed to be objective. This is also a reason why you should be wary of using your own experiences as examples. This is not wrong, but it is clearly subjective and in any case, personal accounts tend to be rather long, distorting the focus of the essay. You should also try to copy the style used by economists. Academic essays are formal, so you should avoid 'journalese'. The *Economic Review* is a good source of sample essays. When writing economics essays you need to use technical terms. It is also a good idea to use diagrams where appropriate. These should be carefully drawn and labelled, for example, give each diagram a title, label the axes, give the units (for example '£') and state the source where necessary. Good textbooks contain many examples of how to draw diagrams.

Another point about style. It should be written in good English – though there can be disagreement about what is acceptable. We began this paragraph by writing a 'sentence' which is not a sentence because it lacks a verb. That is normally not acceptable, but it has been done deliberately to make the point that rules can sometimes be broken. In general, however, good English and accurate spelling and punctuation are desirable because without them it is more difficult to read your essay. If your English is not very good, two suggestions may help. The first is to use spellcheck if you are using a computer. If you do this, make sure that you also read and check what you have written. Computer spellchecks are very useful, but they may let errors go through because the word is spelt correctly, even though it is not the correct word. (In the last paragraph I typed 'god practice' instead of 'good practice'. The computer thought that this was correct.) If you are handwriting your essay, then use a dictionary to check all the words that you are not sure about.

The second suggestion is to read your essay aloud. What may seem all right on paper will sound odd when you read it aloud, and so make you look more closely at what you have written. This technique works even better if you read aloud to a friend who can help point out poor English. It is good academic practice to get others to read and comment on your writing. If you look at the beginning of this book, you will see that it has been read and commented on by several other people. This improves the content of what we have written, but it is still our responsibility.

One final point – pay careful attention to departmental guidelines for essays. These may include specific requirements and give helpful suggestions, including dates and method of submission and whether or not they have to be produced on a computer. If this is the case, allow time for computer breakdown and print queues.

▶ Summary – the steps in writing an essay

- The essential first step is to read and think about the essay title. What does it mean? What are the essential points – the focus of an answer?
- Gather material for an answer. This might involve quite a long period in the library. Make sure that you start early, so that you have a

greater chance to obtain books that may be in short supply. Record your sources accurately.
* Organise the material into a plan. Make very sure that your plan really does focus on the specific question.
* Write a first draft, making sure that every sentence helps to develop your argument.
* Review your draft. Does it focus on the specific question? Can you leave out parts, or do you need to add material? If possible, get a friend to review your draft. Check spelling and punctuation.
* Write the final draft.

Most important of all, allow enough time for the process.

References

Purvis, R. (1994) 'Writing essays', in Saunders, D. (ed.) *The Complete Student Handbook*, Oxford, Blackwell.
Redman, P. *et al*. (1998) *Good Essay Writing. A Social Sciences Guide*, Milton Keynes, Open University.

Further reading

Dunleavy, P. (1986) *Studying for a Degree in the Humanities and Social Sciences*, Basingstoke, Macmillan.
Northedge, A. (1990) *The Good Study Guide*, Milton Keynes, Open University.
Peck, J. and Coyle, M. (1999) *The Student's Guide to Writing*, Basingstoke, Macmillan.

Appendix

Abbreviations and foreign language words

Very often in you are reading you will see various abbreviations used. You may also wish to use these. This list is not meant to be complete, but a useful summary.

cf.	*(confer)* compare
ch.	chapter
ed., ed(s)	editor(s)
e.g.	*(exempli gratia)* for example
et al.	*(et alia)* and others (usually after an author's name)
ibid.	*(ibidem)* the same (as the last reference) This saves writing out the reference again

i.e.	(*id est*) that is
op.cit.	(*opera citata*) in the work recently cited. This saves writing a full reference to a work you have already listed. For example, (Jones 1999, op. cit.) refers the reader back to this work by Jones
p., pp.	page, pages
(sic)	usually indicates that there is something wrong or odd about the original source. For example, if you were quoting someone writing about good English who made a bad grammatical error, you could point this out by putting (sic) after the error.
Tr.	Translator
Vol.	Volume

Source: Adapted from Redman, P. *et.al*. (1998) *Good Essay Writing: A Social Sciences Guide*, Milton Keynes, Open University.

8 Assessment

This chapter will help you to get better grades. There are, of course, many types of assessment: for example, essays, multiple-choice, data response questions, unseen exams, numerical exams, open book exams, and assessed presentations. We cannot cover all these in detail, so we will concentrate on the typical unseen written exam whilst giving hints about some other forms of assessment.

▶ Why exams?

Few people like exams. They are a very imperfect way of measuring student knowledge and abilities and luck can play a major part in determining success or failure; sometimes the questions you have prepared will appear on the exam paper, but sometimes you will be unlucky.

However, exams do have several virtues. They help to pull the course together. Very frequently revision can help students see how different parts of the course fit together, and without exams, few students would revise. Then they are a way in which students can show that they can work under pressure – a valuable ability.

Examinations became popular at the end of the nineteenth century as a way of measuring merit as opposed to influence, and they still have that virtue, particularly in those examinations where students are identified not by name but by anonymous number. This means that tutors mark them without personal prejudice. Another virtue is that it is much harder to cheat in exams than in other forms of assessment.

Whatever their advantages and disadvantages, exams are here to stay; and good technique can help you do well.

▶ Beginning revision

There is one fundamental reason for revising: it will help you do well in the exam. A few students are lucky, they manage to understand and remember the course as they go along, and are clever enough to be able to do well with very little revision. Unfortunately, not many of us are like that. By the end of the course, we have half forgotten what came at the beginning, so we need to revise well.

Organise your time

We have often stressed the importance of organising your time, and this is particularly important in the case of exams. For other kinds of academic work it is sometimes possible to arrange to hand it in late to tutors (for example, when there are compassionate reasons), but exams are fixed. When the exam comes, you must be ready. So, the first thing to do is to draw up a timetable – yes, yet another timetable.

You need to draw up this timetable several weeks before the exam. A good time to start is often just before the Easter vacation (assuming that your exams are in the summer term). This timetable should take into account several factors. You will need to allow some time for rest and recreation – it is neither possible nor desirable to do nothing but work for several weeks, and even when you are working hard you will need breaks. Also you may have to allow time to complete assignments and to do other academic work such as attending lectures. Also, tutors often hold revision lectures that give guidance about the exam.

A good technique in drawing up a timetable is to work backwards from the date of the exam. Allow a few days just before the exam for going over again topics that you have revised, and also allow some time for contingencies; for example, you may have not been able to keep to schedule and so have got behind in your revision. Then decide how many topics you need to revise for each subject and allocate time for each of these. So, your timetable might look like the one shown in Table 8.1.

You will have to decide the details. Some subjects and topics will need more time than others and you may be interrupted in your plans by unforeseen events; hence the need for at least a week before the exam for contingencies.

Past exam papers

Past exam papers are a very useful source of information and can be very helpful in planning your revision (though you should be aware that new tutors on a course may ask very different questions). In many institutions it is possible to obtain them from the library or from the department office. When you first see a past paper, it may put you off – the questions look intimidating, particularly if you get past papers

TABLE 8.1 REVISION TIMETABLE

Week beginning	Activity
April 1	Collect materials and get organised
April 8	Complete last assignment
April 15	Revise topic a, b and c for subject 1
April 22	Complete revision for subject 1 and do topic a for subject 2
April 29	Complete revision for subject 2
	Etc.
May 13	Contingency week/ten days; final going through of revision notes
May 20	Exams begin

fairly early in the course, but the more you study them and link them to your revision, the more comprehensible they become.

Past papers can help in two main ways. They can be a useful source of active revision – this is discussed below - and they can tell you about the structure of the exam. For example, it is important to know the length of exam. In some exams you will be given ten minutes or so to read the exam paper. This is to help you plan your answers and prevent you rushing into answering without thinking. You need to find out if this is the case in your particular exam. Past papers are a good source of information about coming exams; occasionally they give an idea about the particular questions you might get, but usually they will give you an idea about the number of questions you will have to answer and the amount of choice you will have. Then you need to check how this relates to the structure of the course. For example, are there questions on every part of the course? Do you have to revise the entire course, or will it be better to concentrate your limited time on just parts of the course? If you study past papers carefully, when you enter the exam room you will have a good idea of what to expect, at least in terms of the type of questions.

Two other points can be made about past papers. The first is that you need to look at the wording of questions. We discussed this point in the chapter on essay writing, so it may be useful for you to look back at this. The other point relates to question spotting. In some exams it is quite possible to guess what questions are likely to appear, and you would be foolish not to do this. But it is a procedure full of dangers. All too often, a question appears which the student has not expected.

Then she is in difficulty if she has only revised expected questions. So, try to spot probable questions, but revise other topics as well so that you are not caught out if your hopes are not fulfilled.

You will need to decide for yourself how many topics you need to revise. A very rough guide is that if the typical exam paper makes you choose three or four essays from a list of ten on the paper, you need to revise five or six topics (and perhaps more if the questions are likely to be wide-ranging, covering several topics). But this is only a suggestion and needs to be varied according to the circumstances. This can be difficult because two principles clash. On the one hand, it can be argued that you need to know the entire course; on the other, your time is limited and it may be better to revise several subjects in depth rather than all shallowly. In general, your revision topics should focus first on those areas likely to appear on the exam, and second on those topics where you feel you have greatest understanding. Again, much will depend on the guidance that you get from your tutors, and in some exams you may not have any choice. The underlying principle is clear: revise in a way that relates to the questions.

Organise yourself

Before you get down to actually revising, there are other things that you should do in addition to getting copies of past examination papers. The first is to organise your learning materials. If you are a typical student, these will have been put away in a rather haphazard manner. So, begin by organising them by subject and topic. This can be difficult, for example, where a photocopy of an article is relevant to more than one topic. Thus you may be taking a course on economic policy and another on development economics. In this case an article on (say) inflation in the third world may be appropriate in both. One solution to this is to put a note in one set of course notes referring you to the material in another. Plan your revision, because in the exam term many students go to the library to catch up on work they should have done earlier, so books you may want are out and will only reappear after the exam.

Active revision

In some subjects, you may need to remember a large amount of material; in history, for example, it is probably useful if you can remember some dates. But economics is much more a *way of thinking* than a list of things to be learned. This does not mean that there is nothing that is worth remembering, but it is not the essence of the subject. The implication of all this is that revision for economics exams needs to be *active*; you need to think as you revise. Your learning should be meaningful and thought-provoking. At the end of a session you should feel that you have learned something.

A good way to begin, once you have sorted out all your materials and got copies of past papers, is to draw up a list of topics. In some cases it is useful to go quickly through the whole course, making *extremely brief* notes – little more than the occasional phrase or topic title. The aim of this is to remind you what has been covered in the course. It is very easy to forget in May what you did last October. So, begin by getting an overview of the course. Then select the topics that you want to revise. Now you are ready to begin.

At this stage you need to read carefully through all the material that you have on the topic you are revising. Then make this active. You can do this in a number of ways. One is to make *brief* notes as you go along – your time is valuable, so do not waste it by writing out unnecessary things. A good way to do this is to read a section of your original notes, or a photocopy or chapter of a book, then close the book before making your notes. In this way you will be forced to think about what you are writing, and the notes you write will focus on the main points as you try to identify the main ideas that lie at the heart of the topic that you are revising.

For example, if you are revising something on inflation, you may wish to note down something about definitions, then a line about measurement, then a few points about Friedman's ideas, including any criticisms. Then you could do the same for other theories of inflation and also have a section about the effects of inflation. If you really focus your thoughts, you can do this on two sides of A4. In this way you will distil the main ideas and convert them into manageable forms. You can then put this on one side to go through again when you have a few spare minutes. It is a good idea to get a friend to test you on the ideas that you have noted down. In this way the central points about inflation will be clear in your mind – explaining something to someone else is a very good way of learning.

Another revision technique is to pick a question on your chosen topic from a past exam paper, then write a timed answer; if you have an hour in the exam, sit down for an hour to write an answer. Then review your answer and see how it could have been improved. The advantage of this is that it gives you a good idea of how much you will be able to write in the exam. The disadvantage is that it is time-consuming, and it is very difficult to pluck up energy more than once to write out a full answer. So, an alternative is to write out a plan. This has a number of advantages. It does not take long and it forces you to focus on the heart of the question. Perhaps most importantly, if you do this for two or three questions on each topic, you will see how you need to modify your basic material in order to answer the specific question set.

The procedure you adopt to do this should be very similar to that adopted when planning an answer to a course work essay:

- What does the question mean? A useful tip is to underline the main words in the question
- What theories or concepts are relevant?
- Organise your points into a coherent structure

Try to do all this without looking at your notes. When you have finished, look back at your notes, and see what you could have added; or better still, could you have organised your material differently?

Let us take an example. Suppose that the question is 'Evaluate the government's policy towards monopoly'. There are three elements here: 'monopoly', 'government policy' and 'evaluate', so you will need to write about government policy, and about theoretical aspects of monopoly, and you will need to judge the effectiveness of the government's actions. Hence you need to think about concepts such as barriers to entry, oligopoly, consumer surplus and efficiency as well as specific laws.

Now organise your ideas into a coherent plan. This might be along the lines of :

1. Why monopoly is a problem
2. Aspects of the government's policies: towards single firms, towards oligopolies, and so on (or you could organise round specific problems such as collusion between firms)
3. Evaluate what is good and what are the weak points in the government's policies

Also, at this time, make use of your friends. If your friend is taking the same course, compare your outline answers with theirs. Then discuss the similarities and also the differences. It is also very useful if you can invent questions to test each other on, or try to apply theories. For example, if you are revising unemployment, ask 'What measures should the Chancellor take to reduce unemployment?' A broad question such as this can then be dissected; for example, what are the difficulties in the measures you have suggested? What would critics say?

Ways of remembering

Earlier we said that economics is a way of thinking ·rather than topics to be learned. Nevertheless, it is useful to be able to learn some things off by heart, for example in introductory economics, the factors that might cause a shift in the demand curve, or the formula for elasticity. And it is certainly very useful to be able to remember the things you have been revising.

Now, there is a good deal of psychological research into remembering – far too much to summarise here, but there are some simple techniques that may help you. An obvious one is repetition. Write things out several times. Say them out loud several times. Record them on tape and play it several times

Time and recall is a useful approach. This involves regularly reviewing what you want to learn. For example:

• Revise for about an hour
• Have a break for (say) ten minutes. During this time do something very different
• Write down the main points
• Move on to another topic
• The next day, go over your points again

Note that it is often a good idea to move on to a very different topic. If you try to revise very similar topics together, it is likely that you will mix them up, so that you are not sure what belongs to what (hence don't learn about diminishing returns and diminishing marginal utility together).

In this section we have suggested making notes as a help to remembering. That is fine for many people, but others think better visually, and in any case it is useful to supplement notes with visual representations of what you are learning. For some topics it might be useful to draw ' spider maps' of the kind illustrated in Chapter 6 (p. 125).

Another learning technique is to use mnemonics (from the Greek goddess for memory). There are several ways to do this. One is to use the first letters of words you want to remember to make up a sentence; this need not be very meaningful in itself. For example, if you want to remember the components of aggregate demand (consumption, investment, government, exports minus imports) you could concoct a sentence such as '**C**ome **In** **G**irl, **Ex**orcise **Im**' – very silly, but perhaps helpful. You can probably think up much better ones; in any case, the ones that you make up are likely to be easier for you to remember. A word of warning, however, do not go overboard on mnemonics, or you may end up being unable to remember what the letters represent.

How much you need to remember will depend on the course. Check your tutor's expectations about how much you need to remember; for example, how many facts and statistical data do you need to know?

▶ The exam

There are several things that you can do in the day or two before your exam that will help you do better. The first is to try to be healthy. In other words, do not stay up all night in a desperate attempt to learn something. Opinions differ as to whether or not revision just before the exam is useful – it can muddle your thinking – but it is certain that sleepless nights will worsen your performance. So, try to take some exercise so that you become physically tired before you go to bed.

As far as study is concerned, it is too late to read that book you always meant to, but you can look over your summaries, talk about questions and answers with your friends and generally get mentally organised.

The other thing that you should do is to be prepared administratively. Most important of all, check the dates, times and places of your exams. It is not uncommon for students to turn up on the wrong day, or appear in the afternoon for a morning exam. If this should happen to you, tell your tutor at once; sometimes it is possible to make exceptional arrangements. It is also fairly common for students to *think* that they know where the exam is and to turn up and find that it is in a hall somewhere else. You also need to make sure that you have all the materials that you need. Take two or three pens that you like writing with, so that if one runs out, you are still OK. In economics exams, you may need to draw diagrams, so you will need a couple of pencils and a rubber. Get all these together the day before the exam. In some exams, you are allowed to take in drinks; if this is the case, and you think it might be helpful, then be prepared before the exam day.

On the day of the exam, get to the examination room in plenty of time. It is dreadful if you have to rush to make it on time because your transport arrangements have gone wrong. You should aim to go into the exam room not relaxed – you need your adrenaline flowing – but organised and unruffled.

In the exam

The first thing that you should do is to try to compose yourself. Familiarise yourself with your surroundings and lay out your pens and your drink (if you have one). Then check the instructions on the paper. These will probably be the same as those you are expecting, but you need to make sure. You will lose marks if you expect to answer three questions because that has been the pattern in the past but the actual paper now asks for four. The next thing to do is to read the actual questions. Here you may give a sigh of relief; the questions that you hoped for are on the paper! If you are unlucky, then you will have to work a bit harder to do well. As you look through the paper, tick those questions that you think are possible. If there is a question that looks difficult on one of the topics that you have revised, do not despair. Sometimes all that is needed is for you to 'unpick' the question. If you think about it a bit, you may find that the material that you have revised can easily be adapted to fit the question. On a straightforward exam paper with simple instructions (for example, 'Answer any three questions from a list of ten') this stage should take five minutes or so. In some examinations you might be allowed a few minutes to read the paper to do these things before you are permitted to start writing.

Advice differs about the order in which you should answer questions. Some people say that you should begin by answering a question that is not your best. The rationale is that if you answer this satisfactorily, then you can really have a go at your best question. However, it is probably best for you to begin by answering a question that you can do well. This gets you off to a flying start, and you will have marks in the bag.

Time

Time management is all-important in examinations. All too frequently, students spend far too long on the first couple of questions, so that they have only a few minutes for the last one. Now the notion of diminishing returns is a familiar one for economists, and one of the great truths about exams is that it is very easy to get the first few marks on any answer. However, it gets progressively more and more difficult to get extra marks. If each question is marked out of a hundred, then the first thirty or so marks will be awarded for relatively few points, but to move from 70 per cent to 80 per cent is very difficult. This means that even if your answer is flowing, it is inefficient to spend too long on the first question. So before you go into the exam, you should have a time plan in your mind. If the exam is due to last three hours and you have to answer four questions you will have three-quarters of an hour for each question. It might be a good idea to allow a bit longer for the first question. There are two reasons for this. First, if it is a good question for you, then you will have more to write than on the last question. Second, people tend to write more slowly at the beginning of the exam. By the middle of the session, they are often flowing, so that words come out faster.

The absolutely vital thing is that you should not spend too long on the first question. Allowing fifty-five minutes for reading the paper and answering the first question is a maximum. A good technique is to put your watch in front of you so that you can see it easily. Then on the exam paper jot down the time you need to end the first question. Five minutes before this you need to begin your conclusion to this question.

If you succeed in following your time plan you will maximise your chances of getting high marks. But what if it all goes wrong: you are so carried away that ten minutes or so before the exam ends, you are just about to begin the last answer? What you must *not* do is to spend this vital ten minutes writing an elegant introduction to the answer. You need to show the examiner that you know the material and can adapt it to answer the specific question. This might involve you writing a very brief introduction, then writing numbered points in the form of notes (in sentences), ending with a brief conclusion. If you do this you might scrape a pass mark on this answer but you will certainly get many fewer marks than you would have done if you had written a full answer. So make sure that you do not get into this position; plan your time.

A final word about time. Students often ask: 'How much should I write?' It is impossible to answer this question in terms of the number of words or pages. The answer to this question is: 'You should write as much as you can that is relevant in the time that you have.' This is not an answer that satisfies students who are worried about their ability to write enough, but it is the best approach. And do not get worried about students who keep waving their hands in the air asking for more answer books whilst you are still on the first. All too often these students write pages of irrelevant material in bad handwriting and end up with far fewer marks than someone who has written far less but has produced material that is relevant.

Answer the question
Running out of time is one reason why students do not do themselves justice. The other major fault committed by students in exams is not to answer the actual question. We said earlier that question spotting

could sometimes be useful, but it also can lead to great trouble. This occurs when you are hoping for a particular question, it does not appear, but there is a fairly similar question on the paper. So, the student goes and writes out the answer to the question that they hoped would be on the paper. Result: a lot of irrelevant material. The examiner draws a line through the answer and gives very few marks – perhaps even zero.

The way to avoid irrelevancy is to plan your answer, just as you would in writing a coursework essay, except that in an exam it must be done quickly. There are two ways to do this. If you are happy with the question, and with your knowledge of the material, then all you have to do is to jot down a few words in the order you will answer the question. In an exam, your essay plan should be brief; we have seen essay plans that took up a page or more – a great waste of time. The purpose of a plan is to structure your answer, so in your plan you need not write in sentences where a word or phrase will remind you what to write. You can write your plan on the answer paper, and then draw a line through it. The examiner will not read it – though it will show the examiner that you have thought about your answer. You will not lose marks by having a crossed-out plan in your answer book. So, it may look like this:

1. The theme of my answer
2. Point a
3. Point b
4. Point c
5. Conc.

Then go to it!

However, in some exams it will not be as easy as this. You may have a few ideas but not many; in a few cases your mind may be a complete blank. When this occurs, a useful approach is to forget the actual question for a minute and instead think about the topic. Where in the course does it appear? Then try to visualise *any* material for that part of the course. Jot down anything that you remember. This is a form of brainstorming and one idea often leads to another. The points may not all be relevant to the answer, so when you have got several points jotted down you need to structure these into a plan as described above.

So, the main point of writing a plan is to make you answer the specific question and not the one you hoped would be on the paper. Relevance is all-important! There are other benefits of jotting down a brief plan. One is that it gives a clear structure to your answer; it will not be just a list of semi-connected points, but will develop a real argument. The other advantage is that it is likely to stop you being in the position of starting an answer, and then after ten or fifteen minutes realising that you have run out of things to say.

Good presentation can help you gain marks. It is difficult to produce your best handwriting in an exam, but you should try to make sure that what you write is clear. Examiners are human and, faced with a huge amount of marking, they are less than impressed if they have to struggle to read what you have written. A useful idea is to leave a line at the end of each paragraph so that you have a little space to add brief points if you remember them later. Similarly, it is a good idea to start each new question at the beginning of a new page.

After the exam
When you leave the exam, try to forget about it. The worst thing that you can do is to compare what you have written with that produced by your friends. You will almost always find that they have written something that you have not and so make you worried. This is not a good way to leave an exam, and, in any case, what matters is not so much the number of points that you have made, but rather the quality of argument that you have constructed.

In the meantime, your lecturer will have collected the answer papers. Procedure varies between institutions, but in many the papers will be cross-marked by a second lecturer in order to maintain consistency. Then a sample – sometimes all scripts – will be sent off with examples of coursework to an external examiner – an expert in the field from another institution. The external examiner will mark this sample. This gives an independent view and helps to maintain equality of standards across different institutions. If only a sample is sent it will usually contain all failing scripts, some of the best and a cross-section of the rest. There is then a meeting between internal and external examiners at which final marks are agreed. At this meeting students' special circumstances are taken into account. For example, if a student has a doctor's note saying that at the time of the exam she was ill, this will be taken into account. This also applies to long periods of absence due to illness prior to the exam. Personal circumstances are also considered when these may have led to poor performance. For example, family bereavement may prevent students from doing themselves justice. If any of these applies to you, check the regulations in your institution and make any relevant information available to the examiners.

► Multiple-choice questions

So far in this chapter we have focused on traditional unseen essay-type examinations. However, these are often supplemented by other types of examination, and in economics multiple-choice questions are often used. One reason for this is that they test slightly different abilities than essays do; for example, they can test knowledge of the entire course better than essays. This means that if you are taking a multiple-choice exam, you have to revise the whole course rather than picking and choosing likely topics. Moreover, marking essays can take up a lot of time. As student numbers rise, alternatives are sought and multiple-choice questions offer considerable time advantages to lecturers when there are large numbers of students. They take a long time to construct, but they can often be used again in subsequent years and can be computer-marked. So, one hint is to try to obtain past copies of multiple-choice questions. You may get some of the exact questions and be able to remember the answer! That is possible but not very likely since (a) the institution will often have a large number of questions to choose from and (b) it is difficult to remember many answers – even if you know the correct one. Since they are often computer-marked, it is important to follow the instructions correctly. If they say 'tick in the correct box' this is what you must do, since computers will not be able to 'read' your answer if you do something else such as underlining the correct answer.

A good technique is to go through the questions fairly quickly. You should usually find some where the answer is clear to you. Answer these and then go on to the next. If you have done this, then you will be left with two groups. In some cases you will have a good idea about the answer and be able to eliminate a couple of alternatives, but be unsure about the others. In this case you need to think for a bit. One hint in this position is to draw a quick diagram; this often helps to clarify your thinking. It is often a good idea for you to clarify in your own mind the reasons why you think one answer is correct and why you reject others.

If you have done this and are still unsure, there is another hint: if all else fails, choose the longest answer! The reason for this is that it is comparatively difficult to write correct answers. They must be precisely correct, and that often means more words. This is far from being universally true, so it is only a tip to be used if all else fails.

Let us unpick a typical question:

The demand curve for a factor of production will shift to the right as a result of

A   a fall in the price of the factor
B   a rise in the price of the factor
C   a fall in the price of a substitute factor
D   a rise in the price of a substitute factor
E   a fall in the price of the output.

The first step is to understand the question. It is about factors of production such as labour. And it involves a shift in the curve. So, draw this (quickly). Figure 8.1 illustrates the position. This will show that the firm will employ more of the factor, so answer E is clearly wrong – if the price of the product falls, firms will employ less of the factor of production. So is answer B – if wages rise, firms will tend to employ fewer workers, not more. The other alternatives *seem* as if they may be correct, but A and B mean a movement along the curve, not a shift of the curve. Hence, we can conclude that *D* is the correct alternative. A rise in the price of a substitute factor, such as capital, will mean a shift in the demand curve for labour and more workers will be employed. Note that in answering this, as with many questions, a very quick diagram will help.

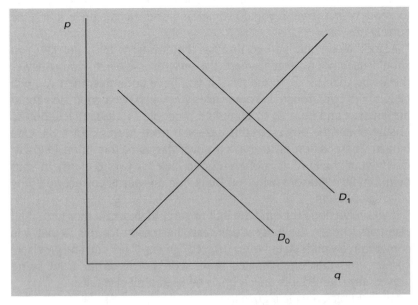

FIGURE 8.1   A SHIFT TO THE RIGHT IN DEMAND FOR A FACTOR

Two other points about multiple-choice questions. Time is again important, so you should keep an eye on the clock. The reason for answering the easy ones first is to make sure that you are not left at the end of the exam with no time but with questions that you could have answered. So, do not agonise too long about a particular question; make sure that you finish. The other point is that you need to check the regulations. In most multiple-choice examinations, you are not penalised for wrong answers. In this case, you must answer all the questions, even if you are unsure of the answer. In some examinations, however, wrong answers are deducted from correct answers. In this case, you should not guess at answers unless you are fairly sure of the correct answer.

▶ Data response questions

'Data' in this context do not just mean statistical data; they can come in a variety of forms such as an extract from a newspaper or government report. Data questions are often designed to see if you can *apply* your knowledge to a particular area. For example, if you are given data about the size of firms in the car industry, you may need to apply concepts such as economies of scale or oligopoly.

Almost all that we have written above applies to data response questions. Try to get hold of past questions or books containing data response questions and use these to practise. Read the question very carefully. Then try to think what concepts or theories may be relevant. Very often you will need to think carefully before you answer. That is because lurking behind the actual words may be a requirement for you to apply a particular theory that may not be immediately apparent. Hence you need to think about what lies behind the data. It is not enough to summarise the material (unless the question asks you to do this); you will usually need to put it into a theoretical context.

Again, let us unpick a question.

Draw diagrams to illustrate the effect on UK price levels and real GDP of the following changes, assuming that the economy is below full-employment GDP.

A   Quantity of money (£M4)

1992	1999
507 billion	790 billion

B   UK average weekly earnings (male)
1981   1998
£125   £384

A: Assuming *ceteris paribus*, an increase in the quantity of money will increase aggregate demand, since people will have more money to spend. The effect is shown in Figure 8.2. The result is a rise in prices and in GDP.

B: This is a bit more complicated, since there may be two effects. Again, assuming no change in other factors, a rise in earnings that is not accompanied by rises in productivity will shift the short-run aggregate supply curve upward. The result will be a rise in prices and a fall in output as shown in Figure 8.3. You could add an important concept here, by saying that the reason is a fall in workers' marginal revenue product compared to their costs.

The complication arises because the rise in wages might also lead to a rise in aggregate demand. This would lead to the result shown in answer A.

This answer specifically asks for a diagram, but this is often good procedure even when it is not requested. Also, think what concepts you might use. These strengthen your answer.

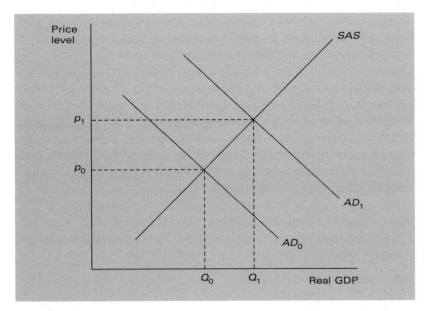

FIGURE 8.2   THE EFFECT OF AN INCREASE IN THE QUANTITY OF MONEY

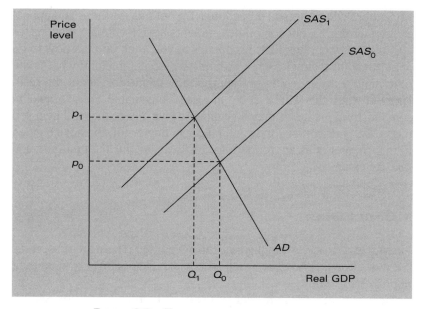

FIGURE 8.3   THE EFFECT OF A RISE IN EARNINGS

► Coping with stress

Examinations are stressful to almost all students. There are several suggestions that can help you cope with this. They will not eliminate stress, but some stress can be a good thing since it may stimulate you to act and give you an impetus to revise. But stress can also be destructive, making you ill or so depressed that you find it hard to work.

So, try to think positively. Make positive statements to yourself. What are your virtues? Also try to mix studying with exercise. Go for a swim, jog or walk as fast as you can for half an hour.

If you are feeling very stressful, make use of your institution's support system. These can be very helpful. In some cases, your personal tutor may be able to help; in others you may find it better to talk to the institution's professional counsellors – though these will probably be very busy at exam time.

► If you fail

Find out when the results of your exams are published, and be there. Then if the worst comes to the worst you can take action. All is not lost, since there will be appeal procedures. Do not misuse these and appeal for trivial reasons, but sometimes students have legitimate reasons for appealing. If you think that this applies to you, then find out how to go about this; for example, what grounds are acceptable and what is the time limit. If an appeal is not appropriate, then think about the resit. Find out when this will be and if any help is available. For example, in some institutions tutors may be willing to give advice that will help you pass. Also, ask yourself why you failed. In any event, the advice given in this chapter is as appropriate for resits as it is for the first time you take an exam.

▶ Conclusion

Passing exams is a technique that can be learned. There are no secrets, but it is surprising how many students make elementary errors in their approach to exams.

The essential points are that you should 'be prepared' – the Scouts' motto is very appropriate so far as exams go. So begin your preparation early enough, draw up a timetable and try to keep to it. Organise your revision and talk about it to your friends. Make brief notes and plan answers to past questions. In the exam, watch the time – spending too long on the first question is a very common way to lose marks. Plan your answers and make sure that you answer the actual question asked and not the one you hoped would be there. Once the exam is over, forget about it.

Further reading

Acres, D. (1994) *How to Pass Exams without Anxiety*, 3rd edn, Plymouth, How To Books.

Cottrell, S. (1999) *The Study Skills Handbook*, Basingstoke, Macmillan.

Dunleavy, P. (1986) *Studying for a Degree*, Basingstoke, Macmillan.

Northedge, A. (1990) *The Good Study Guide*, Milton Keynes, Open University.

9 Writing Dissertations and Projects in Economics

▶ Why dissertations?

A research project is normally an extended piece of work done towards the end of a course. A dissertation can be defined as an original piece of research. The precise requirements vary between institutions, but whatever the exact regulations, they have several features in common. In the first place, dissertations involve research in its sense of 'searching out'. In other words, you have to find out about something. Next, a good dissertation is original – the work that you produce will be different from that of anyone else, even if others choose the same topic. Finally, at the end of your investigation, you have to produce a report – to tell people what you have found out. This involves giving your conclusions, but it also means that you have to show how you have arrived at them, and also point out the limitations of your investigation.

Despite the common features, dissertations can vary considerably. Some institutions require their students to write small-scale dissertations. These have many features in common with a long essay in that the length is shorter than a full dissertation and the topic is chosen for the student. Answering this type of dissertation requires many of the skills used in preparing a 'proper' dissertation. At the other extreme comes a research thesis, usually for a higher degree. Again, many of the skills are the same, but at a higher level, and there will be more emphasis on empirical work in an uncharted area. This lies outside the scope of this chapter which focuses on the kind of dissertation often undertaken in the final year of a degree course where students are asked to write (say) ten or fifteen thousand words on a topic of their own choice.

There are several reasons why dissertations are a common requirement on degree courses. They require a wide range of skills that are often not fully needed in a traditional essay or exam. For example:

Process skills
Assessing information
Library searching
Use of literature
Data collection
Data interpretation
Developing arguments

Presentational skills
Word-processing
Language
Report writing

Personal skills
Independent work
Time management
Project planning
Working to deadlines

Of course, the precise skills that are required will depend on the topic and the institutional guidelines so that not all of these will be needed in every dissertation. On the other hand some dissertations will need other skills. For example, some research projects in economics require mathematical analysis, whilst others will not.

Dissertations can also be useful to students. To some extent luck plays a part in exams – do the questions you want come up on the paper? Dissertations avoid this and will give you a chance to explore an interesting topic at length, though this means that you have to be careful to choose a suitable topic.

▶ Producing your dissertation

Check your course requirements
Before doing anything else, it is a good idea to check the requirements for your particular course. For example, do you need to generate your own data, or is it sufficient to analyse existing data? Similarly, there may be a requirement to use econometric/statistical techniques. And in many institutions tutors are very willing to comment on students' draft materials. If this is the case in your institution, take advantage of the offer.

Make up a timetable

Writing a dissertation takes a long time, so you need to allow for this. Much of the time will not be spent actually writing up your research but waiting for books or replies to letters. So, think ahead and sketch out a rough timetable.

The starting point for this will be your departmental guidelines. These will give you much useful information, for example, how it will be assessed. They will probably also include a date by which your dissertation must be handed in. In many institutions, this is rigid and many marks will be lost if you do not meet this date. A timetable should allow you to meet the deadline and it also forces you to think about the jobs that you will have to do to complete your work.

In completing your timetable you need to allow for things outside your control which may delay you. For example, it may need to be typed and if you cannot do this yourself you may have to wait till your typist has time to fit you in. Again, you may be ill, or have to wait for others to reply to your enquiries. So, make allowance for all this at the beginning.

Your timetable will be personal to you and your institution. Table 9.1 is therefore just a rough guide that needs to be adapted to your particular needs.

This timetable assumes that your report needs to be presented in April; if you have a different deadline, yours will be different. Note that

TABLE 9.1   A POSSIBLE DISSERTATION TIMETABLE

Job	Weeks allowed	Schedule
Find guidelines, produce timetable	1	June
Choose a topic	2	June
Literature search	$1^{1}/_{2}$	June/July. Then holiday
Research design	1	September
Collecting data	4	October/November
Analysing data	3	November/December
Writing first draft	2	January
Second draft	1	February
Typing/binding/Time allowed for emergencies	3	March
Hand in dissertation	–	April

the weeks in this timetable will not be full weeks, since you will have to be doing other things in this period.

One other point. If your dissertation is a major piece of work and an important part of your degree, then try to start a year ahead. It is a good idea to talk over your possible topics with your tutor before undertaking extensive research. Moreover, starting a long time before submission is required allows you time to think about the topic, and it means that you can do some jobs, such as ordering journal articles and books from other libraries before the summer vacation. This means that they will be ready for you on your return to the university after the vacation (though be careful – most inter-library loans have to be returned by a due date, and it is possible that books you have ordered will have arrived for you and been returned by the institution by the end of the long vacation).

Choosing a topic

For most students, this is one of the most difficult problems. A few lucky people will have a lifelong interest in a particular topic and will jump at the chance to explore it in some detail, but for most people choosing a topic is full of uncertainties. If you choose a poor topic, you may have to spend a long time on something that you find boring, or worse; for example, you may find that you cannot obtain data and so become stuck halfway through. That is why it is important to undertake preliminary research to make sure that material is available.

There are three main steps to choosing a suitable topic:

1. *Choose a topic that interests you.* This is rather obvious, but essential. There are several ways to approach this. One is to build on the options that you have chosen as part of your course. For example, if you are taking an option on social economics that you find interesting, then choose a topic such as poverty. This will have an added benefit since your work on the dissertation may also be useful on the option. Similarly, if you are taking another subject such as history, then think about an economic history topic. If you are also taking mathematical options, then a topic using mathematics might be very suitable. (This assumes that your department guidelines give you a free choice; always check before starting serious work on your dissertation.) If you have already enjoyed writing an essay on a particular subject, you may be able to build on this and expand it into a dissertation.

Another approach is to choose a topic where you can draw on

your previous experience. This is particularly apt for mature students who may have specialist knowledge; for example, someone who has worked in a bank prior to college may choose a banking topic. Similarly, if you have an interest in the environment, then a topic on environmental economics would be a good choice. A variation of this is to choose a topic that you think might be useful in the future. If you are hoping for a job in (say) the tourist industry after graduating, then a topic relating to this industry may be interesting and also helpful in getting you a job.

2. *Do some preliminary research.* It is often a good idea to have two or three possible topics in mind at first in case further investigation suggests that there may be insurmountable difficulties in some areas. So, you need to do some preliminary research and find out a bit more on your probable area of investigation. The approach suggested in the chapter on writing essays (pp. 130–46) is one way to begin this. Also, see if there are any journals on the topic and talk to a librarian about your alternatives. You can also take some of the steps discussed below on doing a literature search. The important thing is to make sure that you will be able to complete your dissertation satisfactorily.

3. *Narrow your topic.* It is extremely difficult to write a good dissertation on a broad topic. All too often students have an interest in an area, choose the whole of this area, and then end up writing broad generalisations or a descriptive survey. Students are often reluctant to narrow their topic because they are afraid that they will not be able to find enough material. This is unlikely, and your preliminary research should show this. A broad topic might be suitable for a book, but a good dissertation should develop an argument – a thesis – and this is much easier if it is a narrow area. For example, if you are interested in the car industry, then narrow it down into an investigation into (say) imports in the UK, or labour relations or the recent history of one firm or competition in industry in the UK. You may then be able to narrow the topic even more.

Once you have narrowed down your choice, then go and see your dissertation supervisor. Put down on paper an outline of what you have done and intend to do and ask for comments and help. Most tutors are very happy to help students who are willing to work hard; what they dislike are students arriving at the last minute with little idea of what they want to do. At this meeting you can also agree when you should meet again and see if your supervisor is able to comment on your draft proposals. It is often also very helpful to look at past dissertations. These are often available in the department, either held by tutors or in the library. They can give you ideas on topics and, presentation and give you a feel of what is required.

Literature review

Once you have decided on a topic, the next step is to undertake a literature review; that is to find out what others have written on the subject. There are several reasons for this:

- as a vehicle for learning where you build on your knowledge of the subject
- to facilitate your research. What you read will influence your research design
- as a summary of what has gone before.

Three very important factors should be borne in mind before you start your literature search. The first is *time*. This has been discussed already. The second factor is *accuracy*. If you are making notes, then they must be accurate. Good economics is precise, and rough-and-ready surveys are not much use. In particular, take great care with your references. If you are making notes on material that you will have to hand back to the library, then you need to have full details, such as date of publication and page number, before you return the material. This is a good time to decide on the referencing system that you will use. The departmental guidelines may instruct you on this.

The third factor is perhaps less important. A good literature search reveals *what is known now*. A survey from a textbook a decade old will indicate to your tutor that you have not done much work. It may be a good starting point, but not a good finishing point. Your starting point for your literature search will probably be books. These have the advantage that they are often easily available and are relatively easy to find (as compared, say, to an article in an obscure journal). So the library catalogue is probably where you will start. Then move on to a book called the *British National Bibliography* or *BNB* as librarians call it. This is available in paper form, on CD-ROM and online. In paper form it appears weekly, so is very up to date. Books are listed according to subject, using the Dewey system described in Chapter 7. If books are listed that would be useful, but are not in your library, then ask your library to borrow them for you. (But note that it costs libraries to borrow from others, so some put limits on the number you can order. One way round this is to use your local library as well as your academic library.) Another useful source of information about books is *Whittaker's Books in Print*. This provides details of books published in the United Kingdom and some English language titles published in continental Europe. *Books in Print* covers books published in the USA. Both *Whittaker's Books in Print* and *Books in Print* are available on CD-ROM.

In addition to the above, there are specialised lists of books. For example, there is an *International Bibliography of Economics* that includes periodicals as well as books. This is also available via the online system called BIDS. One disadvantage of bibliographies is that they take time to compile and so do not include the most recent work.

A good literature search will include work published in journals; indeed, they may well be the most important source. They have the advantage that they are often more up to date and in touch with recent debate. Again, your starting point should be your library where the journals will be stored in topic order, probably using the Dewey system. The next step might be to use the *Journal of Economic Literature*. This has major survey articles and also lists recent journal articles using its own classification scheme (that is, it does not use Dewey). Anbar is another useful source. It is an abstracting service covering about 300 international journals. It is available on paper and CD-ROM. The *Business Periodicals Index* is also available on CD-ROM as well as paper and covers American as well as major British journals. Be careful in using American sources; you might find nothing under 'labour' since material will be listed under 'labor'. Newspapers are another good source of material in economics. There are printed indexes to the major UK newspapers, and the *British Newspaper Index* lists summaries of articles and is available on CD-ROM. However, it is not easy to read.

The Internet is a growing source of information about economics. Stein (1999) is a very good source of information about the Internet and includes a chapter specifically devoted to resources for economists. It also has a chapter on European Union sources. There is not space here to go into the use of the internet as a source, but the best starting point is the Biz/ed website which is an information gateway for students and teachers of economics and business (www.bized.ac.uk/). Newspapers are another useful source. You can find material from the *Financial Times* at www.ft.com, from the *Guardian* at www.guardian.co.uk and from *The Economist* at www.economist.com/. The OECD publishes issue-based articles and international data at www.oecd.org/. You can find European material on the European Union website at http://europa.eu.int/index-en.htm, and another useful European site, this time also giving information on third world countries and such issues as globalisation can be found at www.oneworld.org/euforic (euforic stands for Europe's Forum on International Cooperation). The International Monetary Fund also publishes material at www.imf.org/external.htm. Information on international trade matters can be found at the site of the World Trade Organisation: www.wto.org/. Information about international labour can be found at the International Labour Organisation's site: www.ilo.org/ whilst the Office for National Statistics offers both micro and macro time series data at www.ons.gov.uk/ons_f.htm. Finally, a very useful site is that of the Treasury. This can be found at www.hm.treasury.gov.uk/. As might be expected, this provides lots of information about the performance of the UK economy, but it also reviews topics such as European economic integration.

Other sources can be briefly mentioned. Government publications are often essential. These cover a huge area, and are often difficult to locate, so ask a librarian. There is an official list of government publications. A monthly publication, *Economic Trends*, is the best single source of statistical data in economics for the UK. It has an Annual Supplement that gives more detail, including tables going back several years. Finally, you may need to look at information provided by companies. The *Directory of British Companies* provides basic information on all limited companies.

There is not space here to provide a detailed guide to the many sources of information. The best source, which we have used extensively here, is a chapter by Ironfield (1998). This is full of useful information.

Research design

Once you have decided your topic and done some preliminary reading, you need to plan how you will do your research. The exact plan will depend on your topic. For example, a mathematical thesis might require some data collection and then a considerable amount of mathematical analysis. However, the first step is to move from a general topic to an investigation: in other words to clarify the purpose of your research. In many cases it is useful to begin by writing down a paragraph that states what you hope to find out. This will enable you to focus your work.

Let us give an example. Suppose that you are interested in investigating the relationship between education and economic growth in developing countries. This might have developed out of a module you have studied on economic development. Your purpose statement might read:

> The purpose of this investigation will be to examine the relationship between levels of education and the rate of economic growth in developing countries. Levels of education will be measured by using data on literacy and also on attendance at primary and secondary levels. GNP statistics will be used to measure economic growth and the study will be limited to countries with GDP per capita of less than $1000. Other variables that affect growth, such as democratic structure, openness to trade and relative size of government will also be considered. Regression analysis will be used to identify and measure relationships.

You will notice that this statement identifies the unit of analysis. in this example it is all countries with GDP per capita of less than $1000. You will often need to narrow this down to make your investigation more manageable.

The next step is to develop a theoretical framework. In some cases this will be a theory that interests you. Thus if you have become interested in Marxian economics, then you might want to use this as a basis for examining some aspect of unemployment. Similarly, you might use the quantity theory to examine a particular aspect of inflation. However, it is often more useful to use a much narrower theory, for example game theory or a theory of markets, as a basis of your investigation.

In planning your purpose of research, you may find it useful to develop one or more hypotheses. For instance, in the example just discussed, you might clarify this by testing the hypothesis that more education leads to higher levels of GNP. Alternatively, you might examine other hypotheses such as:

- that women are less likely to be promoted than men in x industry
- that unemployment is closely linked to levels of education
- that earnings of manual workers have risen more slowly than earnings of nonmanual workers in the last decade

In some cases, particularly in what is called 'phenomenological' research (that is, more philosophical), you might not test a particular hypothesis. Instead you might just develop the purpose of research into a question such as 'An investigation into how workers made redundant in the closure of the XYZ factory in Warrington cope with redundancy'. (This is another example of limiting the scope of your investigation to make it more manageable.)

Once you have done this you need to decide your methodology – how you are going to find out the evidence to answer your research question or to test your hypothesis. In some science subjects, experiments form the usual method of obtaining evidence, but this is an unusual – although growing – technique in economics. If you are interested in this approach, consult Hagel and Roth (1995). A more likely approach is to use a longitudinal study. This involves an investigation of a topic, such as a group of people or a problem, over a period of time. This creates difficulties for students, since it is not possible to follow up groups over a long period of time. Nevertheless, students can do interesting work using this method. For example, if a local firm makes people redundant, it might be possible to question a sample of them at regular intervals over a period of a few months and discover, for example, what factors might be associated with obtaining new employment. This would be the approach to use in an investigation such as the XYZ factory just mentioned. Another longitudinal investigation might be to look at local food prices over a period of time and compare your results with changes in national food prices. This would require mathematical skills.

An alternative approach is to do a cross-sectional study. This involves finding out information on variables in different contexts at the same time. The advantage of this is that the data collection can be done at one time. For example, it might be possible to compare productivity in several countries at a particular moment in time. Since it would not be practicable for a student to collect such data, it would depend on the availability of published data that could then be analysed. An alternative, where it might be possible to collect data, could be to investigate the extent of training in local firms and then try to explain the findings.

Surveys are sometimes used in economic research. This involves taking a sample and using this to make generalisations about a larger group. The redundancy example just mentioned would involve a survey. Similarly, it might be possible to examine the income and spending patterns of students. Alternatively, it might be interesting to investigate the extent of part-time working by students.

Case studies are a possibility. Here the intention is to investigate one situation in some depth and then draw out inferences. For example, it might be possible to examine the impact of your institution on the local economy. Case studies are particularly appropriate when you have contacts – if you want to study a local factory it is helpful if your father owns the factory! A potential problem for case studies is that what is true for one case might not apply to others.

A more philosophical approach might be to take one of the perspectives discussed earlier and apply it to a particular context. Thus a student might take a feminist approach and use this to examine (say) the earnings and status of a group of workers or the importance of non-paid work in the economy.

These suggestions illustrate the wide range of possibilities that students can investigate. It is important not to be too ambitious; taking a very big topic that involves a lot of work might well create problems later on when you find that time is running out. Far better to investigate a small problem with a relatively simple methodology.

Collecting your data

The kind of data that you will need will depend on the type of dissertation that you are writing. Occasionally, dissertations are little more than reviews of the literature, but in some cases, students have to spend a good deal of time collecting their own material. The first step is to think about the kind of information that you will need. This will follow from your research design. It is foolish to spend time collecting information if you do not need it. Time spent thinking ahead is more than repaid by time saved later on. This means that you need to think about what you want to find out before you start active investigation.

It is conventional to divide data into two types, primary and secondary. The word 'data' is a plural. So you should write 'the data show' rather than 'the data shows'. The singular of data is 'datum', so this is the word to use if there is only one. Primary data are most easily defined as data that you collect yourself. For example, if you get people to complete a questionnaire, then this would be primary. So in general would original statistics collected by someone else: for example, government statistics about unemployment or census statistics about population. The distinction is not always clear, however, and some people would count published statistics as secondary. If you take material from published textbooks, then this is clearly secondary data.

Primary data have several advantages. If you are collecting the information yourself, then it will be specific to the problem. Moreover, you will know the limitations and strengths of the information that you have collected. The big disadvantage is that collecting your own data can be very time-consuming and frustrating. For example, you may send out questionnaires to local firms to find out (say) how many trainees they employ or how many apprenticeships they have. This would be useful for an investigation into industrial training. However, you must expect most firms to throw away your enquiry, either because they regard the information as private or because they cannot be bothered. This means that the results that you get may not be reliable – only the firms with a good record in the area may be willing to reply.

Here are a few tips about collecting data. First, try to do a test run. In some cases this will be relatively easy. If you are asking students about part-time work, then draw up a questionnaire and ask your friends to complete it. This will show you such things as ambiguous questions. Next, throw out questions that are irrelevant. People will be more willing to fill in your form if it is short. In order to encourage them, be considerate. Phrase your questionnaire in a way that shows you realise that you are imposing on them and asking a favour. Also, your questions may involve a certain invasion of privacy. This is particularly true if you are asking about sensitive topics. The most obvious of these are questions about money. People regard this as their own business and will almost always be unwilling to reply to your questions. It is also useful to let them know that your dissertation will keep individual responses confidential.

It is sometimes a good idea to have a letter of introduction from your tutor. This will identify you and may help to secure the cooperation of those you want to contact. It will also give your tutor a chance to consider your proposal and comment on it.

One final hint about collecting data. There is a specialised literature on techniques such as selecting a sample and designing questionnaires. If you intend to use such methods, start by consulting books such as Bouma and Atkinson (1995) or Bell (1993).

Secondary data also have their advantages and disadvantages. These are the opposites of those for primary data. Secondary data are usually relatively easy to obtain – often from the library. The big disadvantage is that they may not be quite what you want – they have been collected for other purposes than yours and so may not fit your needs. Moreover, if you make extensive use of secondary rather than primary data when the latter are obtainable, it may cause your tutor to regard your dissertation as less substantial and so you may receive a lower grade. However, by their very nature many dissertations are forced to rely on secondary data, and this is not then a weakness.

We can add two final points about collecting your data. The first is that you should not throw anything away until you have handed in your dissertation. All too often students have decided that something is no longer useful and thrown it away, only to realise later that it would have been very useful. The second point is that you can go on and on collecting data. There comes a time to say 'That's enough', even though you realise that you could do more. Keep your timetable in mind, and start writing your report.

Writing up your report
Much of what we wrote in the chapter on essays is appropriate here, but a dissertation has special characteristics; in particular it is longer and more detailed and should contain much more original work than an essay. Slapdash writing up can spoil good preparatory work, so you need to think through this stage before starting.

There are three stages to writing up your dissertation: pre-writing, the rough draft and the final draft. In practice, however, these three stages overlap, so that, for example, you may have written a rough draft of some of your paper before you have completed the preparatory stage. Similarly, parts of your dissertation may be in the final stage whilst you are still waiting for some material before completing your first draft or you may suddenly discover material that would strengthen part of your essay, even though you have already written that section.

The pre-writing stage is essentially about getting your thoughts in order, and probably the best way to do this is to sketch out a draft outline. This is easier said than done, because it necessitates reviewing all the material that you have collected and putting it into shape. This will take several hours and it is often advisable to set aside a complete morning to reread your material and to think through your argument. What is the essence of your thesis? This can be painful because it implies rejecting material that you have collected. There is often a tendency for students to include data just because they have them. This is a mistake; what you want is to develop a clear line of argument. Sometimes the data that you have collected may mean that your conclusion will be different from the one you expected. Indeed, it may be that your views change as you actually write the report. This can be a sign of a good dissertation since it means that you have learned from your investigation.

The precise structure of your report will depend on your topic. What follows is therefore merely a suggestion.

Your introduction should set the background. This is often the most difficult to write, and there is a case for writing your introduction last.

It should state your topic clearly. One way to do this is to think back to your research questions or hypotheses. The paragraph that you wrote whilst designing your research programme may help.

The next section of your dissertation may be a survey of the literature. This should not be your summary of everything that you have ever read on the topic of (say) unemployment or competition policy. It should be shaped so that it gives the background of what you intend to investigate. For example, if your topic is an examination of wages in the tourist industry, then your literature review will just deal with this. You may have a paragraph on the size of the industry, but descriptive material about tourist destinations would be irrelevant. The purpose of a literature review is to say, 'This is what is already known about the problem I am investigating.' It therefore forms a foundation on which to base your research. In some cases you will decide not to survey the literature in a separate chapter; instead you can report on what is already known as you go through the various sections of your dissertation.

Another section of your report may then deal with the data collection stage of your work. This should describe the methods that you have used; for example, if you have used questionnaires it should describe how these were constructed, and pre-tested and also the details of who completed them, including the response rate.

Then you might discuss the results of your analysis of the data. This may be mathematical. It may be your analysis of the facts that you have discovered.

The final section of your dissertation may then be a conclusion that draws together what you have done – that is, it summarises the main points – and that also shows its significance. One good way to end your dissertation is to refer back to your introduction – to show that you have dealt with the issues you raised there.

Finally, you will have two important sections. You will need a list of references. We discussed this in the chapter on essay writing, but one point can be added. Add to your reference section as you write your dissertation – do not leave it to the end. That is because when you get there you will probably have forgotten some detail. So, as you write about a particular source, add it to the reference section straight away.

Poor references are a common fault of dissertations. Make sure that you have such things as the date of publication, the author's initials and the publisher. Another fault is that students often list things in the references that they have not read. They do this because a long list of references seems impressive. But tutors are not fools, and they will often guess that you have not read something that you have listed. Be honest. If you have read a reference in Smith to earlier work by Jones, then make this clear by writing 'Jones (19xx) etc., quoted in Smith etc.'

Students often try to pass off a direct quotation as their own sentence. This is often a temptation when the original is elegant and relevant, but you must resist the temptation. If you use someone else's words, give them credit. Put the words in quotation marks and give references. And do not plagiarise; this guarantees failure.

You may decide to include one or more appendices. It is often difficult to decide what to put in the main part of your dissertation and what to put in an appendix. The principle is that if it develops your argument, it should go in the main part; if it does not, then the appendix is the proper place. For example, copies of questionnaires and long lists of statistics are essential but do not develop the argument. Hence the appendix is the proper place for them.

A typical way to organise your dissertation might be:

- Introduction
- Data collection
- Data analysis
- Conclusion
- References
- Appendices

Now you are ready to write the first draft of your dissertation. Again, much of what we wrote in the chapter on essay writing is appropriate here. Your first step should be to check again the department's guidelines for dissertations. These may include something about length and also about layout. Then, sort out your notes into the order that you have just decided. This may mean notes on cards, your typed notes, statistics, photocopies and so on. You then need to organise these into a coherent structure – a good rule is that you should know what you are going to write before you start. There is one exception to this, and that is when you are struck by an inspiration – a good idea that comes to you as you write. This may mean changing your structure, or adding a bit to an earlier part, or jotting it down to insert at a later stage.

If you are writing on paper, it is a good idea to leave plenty of space for later additions. You can do this by leaving wide margins and space at the bottom of the page. However, it is much better to use a word processor. This makes it possible to write your rough draft very quickly, without worrying too much about choosing the correct word, or if something is grammatically correct – that can be checked later. If you do use a word processor, make sure that you save your material regularly, and at the end of each session save it on a disk so that if anything happens to the main computer you have a copy. It is extremely upsetting to have nearly finished a long piece of work, only to find that it has all been lost.

Finally, you need to do the final draft. If you can, try to leave time between finishing the draft and revising it. You can be too close to a piece of writing to evaluate it properly. How long you leave will depend on your time schedule, so balance the benefits of getting your dissertation finished in good time with those of allowing yourself a critical assessment of what you have written. If possible, persuade a friend to read through your chapter, seeing in particular if the argument flows. Then read it carefully, always asking yourself, 'Is this needed?', or 'Is the evidence here strong enough?' Be prepared to emphasise the limitations of your research; no investigation is perfect, and it will strengthen your work if you can say, for example, that the sample is small or the response rate is not sufficient to come to a firm conclusion. Finally, read it through to check grammar and spelling. Spellchecker systems on a word processor can do most of this for you, but bear in mind that you also need to check for yourself.

Presentation is important. There is no need to go to extremes and use colour printing (unless your work involves complex diagrams and maps) but all too often student's work is shoddy. Take some time to consider the layout of your work. You have gone to a lot of effort in preparing the dissertation, so make sure that it looks good.

Finally, do not hesitate. There is often a reluctance to hand in your work because you think it could be improved. Be brave. Hand it in and forget about it.

References

Bailey, E. P. and Powell, P. A. (1987) *Writing Research Papers, A Practical Guide*, 2nd edn, *London,* Holt, Rinehart & Winston.

Bell, J. (1993) *Doing your Research Project*, 2nd edn, Milton Keynes, Open University Press.

Bouma, G. D. and Atkinson, G. B. J. (1995) *A Handbook of Social Science Research*, 2nd edn, Oxford University Press.

Hagel, J. and Roth, A. (eds.) (1995) *The Handbook of Experimental Economics*, Princeton University Press.

Hussey, J. and Hussey, R. (1997) *Business Research: A Practical Guide for Undergraduate and Postgraduate Students*, Basingstoke, Macmillan.

Ironfield, C. (1998) 'Finding Out in Economics', in Atkinson, B., Livesey, F. and Milward, B. (eds) *Applied Economics*, Basingstoke, Macmillan.

Stein, S. D. (1999) *Learning, Teaching and Researching on the Internet: A Practical Guide for Social Scientists*, Harlow, Longman.

Index

abbreviations, 145–6
absolute advantage, 43
Austrian economics, 53–5

Belfield, C.R. *et al.*, 10–11
Bell, J., 176
Blackaby, D.H., 9
Blundell, R. *et al.*, 9
Bouma, G. and Atkinson, G., 176

careers, 8–11
ceteris paribus, 17, 19
class, 65–6
command economy, 14
competition, imperfect, 30
consumption,35, 91, 99–102
correlation, 106–9
cost, 26–29
  average, 27
  marginal, 27–29
  opportunity, 13–14
crises, 67–8

data collection, 175–7
  issues, 112–13
  primary and secondary, 176–7
  response, 161–3
demand, 16–19, 89, 92–6
  aggregate, 34–9
demand equation, 19–21, 96, 98
development, 68–9
Dewey system, 134–5
disagreements, 60–2
dissertation, timetable, 167–8
distribution, 31
Dorton, P.J., 9

earnings of economists, 8–11
econometrics, 91
economic indicators, 76–8

economics as science, 56–8
efficiency, 31
elasticity, 23–26
entrepreneur, 13
environmental economics, 69–79
equilibrium, 17, 19, 97–9
essays
  criteria, 130–2
  preparation, 131–2
  structure, 138–40

fallacies, 4, 58–9
feminist economics, 78–87
Friedman, M., 50, 51

Gross National Product (GDP),
  37, 76, 76–7, 89–90

Human Development Index, 77

incomes, 99–106, 112–14
index numbers, 109–12
infant industries, 45, 74
inflation, 51, 151
investment, 35
Ironfield, C., 172

Jackson, T. *et al.*, 77–8
jokes, 4

Keynes, J.M., 4, 50, 52, 53
Kuhn,T., 57–8

lectures, 126–7
literature review, 170–2

macroeconomics, 33–4, 99–106
market
  economy, 15
  failure, 32–3